The Perfect Party Planner

The Complete Guide to Children's Parties

Project Directed by Sue Lewis

Written by Karen Famini, Karen Lange,
　　Vicky Shiotsu, and Rozanne Lanczak Williams

Art Directed by Karen Hanke

Designed by Pam Thomson

Illustrated by Patty Briles and Diane Valko

Edited by Mary Pat Ferraro and Joanne Corker

Crafted by Nancy M. Lang and Pam Thomson

Photographed by Ed Aiona and Bruce Shippee

Published by

LEISURE ARTS®

P.O. Box 55595
Little Rock, Arkansas
72215

Table of Contents

Helpful Hints

A great birthday party can be loads of fun for children AND adults! Here are some practical hints to help you plan the perfect party and make the most of your child's special day.

Allow Time for Planning

Give yourself at least one month to plan all the details of your party. As you decide on the best day and time for the celebration, consider how much time you will need to set up the decorations, props, food, and games. If you think you'll need the morning for preparation, plan your party for the afternoon. Do as much preparation as possible before the day of the party.

Involve the Birthday Child

Involve your child in as much of the party planning and preparation as possible. He or she will be delighted to help plan the theme, guest list, menu, games, crafts, and so on. Your child can make invitations, set up crafts and decorations, and prepare simple menu items. Remember—the reason for the party is to make your child feel special!

Set a Time Limit

If your guests are young children, two hours should be plenty of time for the party. You might schedule three or four games and crafts, a light lunch and birthday cake, and time for present opening. If your party guests are older children, you might allow three hours for the party and plan to include crafts and games that take more time.

Make a Schedule

List what your guests will be doing from the time they arrive until the time they leave. Include activities for guests who are early and a plan for those who are late. Make sure that your first activity doesn't depend on all the guests being there, since children will invariably arrive at different times. Also, be sure to schedule some time for free play. Provide balls, paper, markers, and other items for children to use if they finish eating early or if they are waiting for others to complete an activity.

Have a "Plan B"

Rain or shine, the party will go on! If you're planning an outdoor party, have a backup plan in case of bad weather. Have additional activities available "just in case." Relays, dance music, balloon volleyball, and storytelling are good backups because they require little preparation and they're always a hit.

Get Help

Have a family member, an older child, or a friend assist you with the party. You will need the extra hands to help children with crafts and games. He or she will also free you to do other things, such as restocking food and drinks, or preparing for the next activity. Ask your helper to take photos and/or videos of party highlights.

Prepare Your Home

- Plan a safe, comfortable place for your party. Childproof the area by placing breakables and valuables in another room. Special tables, flooring, and furniture can be covered with decorative sheets or plastic.

- If you have pets, place them in a comfortable area away from the party. Even though pets are considered part of the family, you may have guests who are not comfortable around animals. Also be aware of children who may be allergic to dogs and/or cats.

- Be sure your house or apartment numbers are visible from the street. Balloons or cardboard signs placed near your driveway or street entrance will assist guests in locating the party.

Be Flexible

Remember that your schedule is only a guide. If a game is going extremely well, let children continue playing. If an activity doesn't seem to be working, move on to something else. Keep in mind that children will be excited and mishaps may occur. Even if the party does not go exactly as planned, keep your sense of humor—and most of all, have fun!

Don't Forget the Cameras!

Take lots of photos and videos! You and your child will want to remember this special celebration. Polaroid pictures are fun to take and can be used during the party for various crafts. Regular film can be developed after the party and sent to partygoers in thank-you notes. A good thing to remember is that it's not necessary to have every child in every picture. Candid shots of small groups, pairs, and individuals capture the fun best. And any videos taken during the party can be shown to partygoers while they are waiting to be picked up.

Send Thank-You Notes

Sit down with your child a week or two after the party to write thank-you notes. Craft materials or computer programs can be used to design fun, creative cards or notes. Specialty stores also have a wide variety of cards to choose from. For a special treat, include a photo from the party as a keepsake.

Sleepover Preparations

The Slumber Party and Sleepover chapters of this book are specifically designed to be overnight parties. However, many of the party themes in this book can also be used for sleepover parties.

If you're having a sleepover, you may want to consider these helpful suggestions:

- On the invitations, be sure to include the time the party begins, usually between 5:30 and 7:30 p.m. Be sure to indicate a pickup time the next morning. The invitation should also advise guests about what to bring (e.g., sleeping bag, pillow, toiletries, pajamas, favorite stuffed animal).

- Show a video or read stories as a way to settle down children when it's getting late. Choose stories and videos that fit the theme of the party, and preview videos to be sure they're appropriate for a young audience.

- Save a few snacks and drinks for later in the evening. Children love to curl up in their sleeping bags and snack while telling stories or watching videos. Choose munchies that will not make too much of a mess, and serve drinks in covered containers to prevent spills.

- Flashlights, nightlights, and glow sticks are fun as well as useful for partygoers to have on hand during the night. Making shadow puppets, dancing with glow sticks, and spotlighting various performances are all great nighttime activities. Children will also appreciate having lights for midnight trips to the bathroom.

- Be sure to write down telephone and pager numbers where parents can be reached if needed.

Carnival

Prizes

Clown Straw Pattern

(page 14)

hair

hat

face

Stand-up Clown Pattern

(page 14)

hat

arms (2 per child)

bow tie

hands (2 per child)

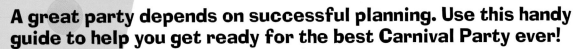

Getting Started

A great party depends on successful planning. Use this handy guide to help you get ready for the best Carnival Party ever!

One Month Before the Party

____ Decide on day, time, and location of party.

____ Write a guest list. (Keep the number manageable.)

Two to Three Weeks Before the Party

____ Buy (or make) and send out invitations. Include an RSVP.

____ Make a list of decorations, food, and activity supplies.

____ Make or buy party decorations (e.g., banners, streamers, hats).

____ Buy and collect items needed for games and crafts.

____ Buy colorful party table items (e.g., paper plates, cups, utensils, tablecloth, napkins).

____ Buy food items that do not need to be refrigerated.

____ Buy prizes (e.g., small toys, fun erasers, candies).

____ Make props (e.g., booths, signs, items for games).

____ Decide on an area for the games, crafts, and gifts.

____ Check batteries and film in camera and video camera.

____ Select background music (optional).

Week of the Party

____ Call any guests who have not responded.

____ Buy last-minute items.

____ Borrow tables, chairs, and other needed items.

____ Prepare foods that can be made ahead of time (e.g., Carnival Cake and Fruit Medley can be made the night before).

____ Make cake or order one.

____ Order balloons.

____ Prepare all craft projects and cut out all patterns. Prepare a bag of materials for each craft.

____ Prepare all games.

Day of the Party

Four hours before

____ Pick up cake (if ordered).

____ Pick up balloons (if ordered).

____ Buy ice for cooler, if needed.

____ Set up party tables.

____ Set up booths, signs, prizes, games, crafts, and decorations.

____ Make Clown Dip.

Two hours before

____ Organize background music (optional).

____ Complete last-minute foods and drinks.

One hour before

____ Make sure your child is dressed for the party and ready to greet guests.

____ Prepare popcorn.

____ Prepare hot dogs.

____ Place chip and pretzels on Clown Dip.

As guests arrive

____ Greet guests and make them feel welcome.

____ Have paper and pen available to write down telephone and pager numbers where parents can be reached if needed.

Clown Straws See directions on page 14.

Carnival Cake

This big, bold clown cake will draw oohs and ahs from any carnival crowd!

Ingredients and Supplies

- cake mix of your choice
- prepared white frosting
- tube of decorator's icing (one or more colors)
- candy (e.g., sprinkles, gumdrops, candy corn)
- 5" Styrofoam ball
- waffle cone or paper cup
- curling ribbon or thin red licorice
- scissors
- tape
- toothpicks
- bundt pan
- cooling rack

Directions

1. Bake the cake in a bundt pan, according to directions on the box.

2. Cool the cake in the pan for 25 minutes. Remove the cake from its pan, and allow it to cool completely on a rack before frosting.

3. Cover the cake with white frosting. Decorate it with candy sprinkles and other trim. (You could store the cake at this point and add the clown's head on the day of the party.)

4. Cut strands of curling ribbon and curl them tightly with scissors. Tape the ribbon hair around the Styrofoam ball. (String licorice may also be used for hair. Secure with toothpicks.)

5. Use gumdrops or pieces of candy corn to make the nose and eyes. Attach them to the head with toothpick halves.

6. Create the mouth with red decorator's icing or licorice secured with toothpicks.

7. Tape three or four toothpicks inside the cone or cup so the points stick out about ½".

8. Use icing and candy to decorate the hat. Add frosting around the rim.

9. Place the hat on the clown's head, pressing the toothpicks into the ball and pushing the hat gently.

10. Place the completed clown's head on the Carnival Cake.

Party Foods

Serve traditional carnival fare such as hot dogs, chips, and drinks. Include these other fun foods for special carnival treats!

Carnival Dogs

Ingredients: hot dogs, hot dog buns, condiments (catsup, relish, mustard, cheese spread)

Directions

1. Microwave, boil, or grill hot dogs, and place them in buns.

2. Set out the condiments and serve the hot dogs from a carnival booth (see page 12). Let the guests help themselves!

Clown Dip

Ingredients and Supplies: 2 cups sour cream, 2 tbsp dry onion soup mix, olives, cherry tomatoes, red peppers, tortilla chips, pretzel sticks, carrot and celery sticks, bowl, small dishes

Directions

1. Mix sour cream and soup mix in a small bowl. Chill the dip for at least two hours.

2. Spoon the dip into small dishes. To turn each dip into a funny clown face, add olives for eyes, a cherry tomato for the nose, a red pepper slice for the mouth, and carrot and celery sticks for the collar. Just before serving, add a tortilla chip hat and pretzel stick hair. Serves 8–12.

Bagged Popcorn

Ingredients and Supplies: microwaved or prepared popcorn, small lunch bags, large box lid, contact paper (two or three colors), scissors

Directions

1. Partially fill lunch bags with popcorn and arrange bags on a tray. (Use a large box lid covered with alternating colors of contact paper.)

2. Ask your helper to be the popcorn vendor and take the tray around.

Carnival Fruit Medley

Ingredients and Supplies: watermelon, cantaloupe, honeydew melon, melon baller, large bowl, knife, spoon, skewers

Directions

1. Cut each melon in half and spoon out the seeds.

2. Scoop out melon balls or cut fruit into pieces. Place fruit in a large bowl.

3. For older guests, serve the melons on skewers, mixing the colors.

Games and

What's a carnival without fun and games?

Carnival Booths

Materials: tables, benches, or large boxes; colorful tablecloths or sheets; bright contact paper; scissors; construction paper; paint; paintbrushes; balloons; streamers; prizes in a container

Directions

1. For each booth, cover a table, bench, or large box with a tablecloth, sheet, or contact paper.

2. Decorate by painting a sign with the booth's name (e.g., Hot Dogs, Penny Toss, Face Painting, Prizes), and then add balloons, streamers, or flags.

3. Place party prizes and treats in a container near the games or at the prize booth.

4. Hand out the prizes after each game. Children can keep prizes in their prize bags.

Prize Bags

Prize Bags, also known as Treat Bags, Loot Bags, Goody Bags, and Take-Home Bags, are important treasures for your party guests. Prizes should suit the age of your guests as well as the theme. Consider stickers, small toys, pinwheels, pencils, fun erasers, candies, and other carnival-related items. Be sure each child receives several prizes.

Materials: white lunch bags, ruler, hole punch, ribbon, scissors, fabric paint, glitter, markers, stickers, party prizes

Directions

Prepare steps 1–3 before the guests arrive.

1. Open each bag and fold the top down twice to make a 1" rim.

2. Punch two holes on one side of the rim, about 1½" from the side edges. Repeat on the other side.

3. Cut two 18" lengths of ribbon. Thread one piece through the two holes on one side of the bag, and knot the ends to make a handle. Repeat on the other side.

4. Set out bags, markers, fabric paint, glitter, and stickers. When guests arrive, have them write their names on the bags and decorate them.

Activities

Get your celebration rolling with some of these wild and wacky carnival activities!

Penny Toss

Materials: five small cans, wrapping paper or contact paper, cardboard or plywood (about 10" x 13"), bright-colored paper, scissors, glue, masking tape, pennies

Directions

1. Cover the cans with wrapping paper or contact paper. Cover the cardboard or plywood with bright-colored paper.

2. Attach small rolls of masking tape to the underside of each can and arrange the cans in a cluster on the cardboard. Press the cans to hold them in place.

3. Place the game on a table and put masking tape on the floor as a starting line. Vary the distance according to the age of the children.

4. Give each guest five pennies, and have children take turns seeing how many coins they can toss into the cans. At the end of the game, children can keep their pennies.

5. Distribute prizes to all children.

Note: Make two games if you have more than eight guests.

Catch the Bead

Materials: 9-oz plastic cups, 30" lengths of yarn, large round beads, permanent markers, stickers, hole punch

Directions

1. Punch a hole near the top of each cup.

2. Provide each guest with a bead, yarn, and a cup to decorate with markers and stickers.

3. Help children thread the yarn through the bead, securing it with a knot. Thread the other end of the yarn through the hole in the cup and tie it tightly.

4. Children can hold their cups with the beads dangling below. Then they jiggle and jerk the cups to make the beads land inside!

5. Distribute prizes to all children.

Bottle Buddies Knock-Down

Materials: three plastic 2-liter soda bottles, three 4" or 5" Styrofoam balls, stickers, colored electrical tape, ribbon, scissors, rubber balls or beanbags

Directions

1. Decorate the plastic bottles with stickers and electrical tape.

2. Cut facial features from electrical tape and press them onto the Styrofoam balls. Carefully screw the balls onto the bottles. Tie a ribbon around each neck.

3. Place the bottle buddies in a line on a table. Then let your guests stand back and try knocking them down with balls or beanbags!

4. Distribute prizes to all children.

Carnival Crafts

Stand-up Clowns

Materials: toilet paper tubes, 4½" x 6" colored paper, colored paper scraps, Stand-up Clown pattern (page 8), scissors, markers, glue, white paper towels, ¼ sheets of newspaper, rubber bands, ½" pompoms

Directions

1. Before the day of the party, trace the patterns onto colored paper and cut out the pieces. Separate the materials into a plastic bag for each child.

2. Help each child glue colored paper (4½" x 6") around a tube. Decorate it with markers or cut paper scraps.

3. Glue the paper hands to the sleeves, and then glue the sleeves to the back of the tube.

4. Crush newspaper to make a 2" wad for the head. Wrap it in a paper towel, and tie it with a rubber band.

5. Push the head into the tube and draw facial features. Glue on a pompom nose.

6. Overlap and glue the edges of the hat to make a cone. Decorate it with markers or cut paper scraps, and glue a pompom on top.

7. Glue the hat to the clown's head and the colored bow tie below the clown's chin.

Clown Straws

Materials: drinking straws, heavy white paper, Clown Straw pattern (page 8), colored paper, craft knife, pencils, scissors, markers, glue

Directions

1. Before the day of the party, copy the pattern for the clown's face onto white paper and cut it out. Copy the patterns for the clown's hair and hat onto colored paper, and cut them out.

2. Help each child glue the hair onto the white circle, and draw the clown's facial features.

3. Decorate the hat and glue it to the head.

4. Cut a small slit near the top of the head and along the mouth, as shown. From the front, push a straw into the top slit down through the bottom slit.

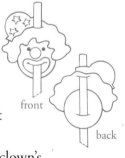
front / back

Masks

Materials: face masks, feathers, sequins, glitter, pompoms, stickers, glue

Directions

Glue decorative items to masks.

Face Painting

Materials: face-painting kit

Directions

1. Purchase a face-painting kit from a party or craft store.

2. Have your helper paint children's faces and/or hands.

If you have room, prepare a separate table with a plastic tablecloth for your craft projects and supplies.

Decorations

Choose colorful plates, cups, utensils, and a tablecloth to
enhance the carnival theme. Add color and excitement to your party table
with balloons, streamers, and confetti. Hang balloons in bunches near the table,
from the backs of chairs, or from a light above the table. Place streamers on the
table or drape them from a string hung above the table. Add any carnival props
you find, such as clown hats, for a festive effect.

To welcome your guests, hang balloons and streamers on the
mailbox and the front door.

Carnival Party Shopping List

Use this handy checklist to help you plan the items you'll need to buy or gather for your party. Check off items as you get them.

Carnival Cake (page 10)
___ cake mix
___ prepared white frosting
___ tubes of decorator's icing
___ bundt pan
___ candy decorations
___ 5" Styrofoam ball
___ waffle cone or paper cup
___ curling ribbon or thin red licorice
___ toothpicks

Carnival Dogs (page 11)
___ hot dogs
___ hot dog buns
___ condiments such as relish, mustard, catsup, and cheese spread

Clown Dip (page 11)
___ sour cream
___ dry onion soup mix
___ olives
___ cherry tomatoes
___ red peppers
___ tortilla chips
___ pretzel sticks
___ carrot and celery sticks

Bagged Popcorn (page 11)
___ small lunch bags
___ microwaved or prepared popcorn
___ large box lid
___ contact paper (two or three colors)

Carnival Fruit Medley (page 11)
___ watermelon
___ cantaloupe
___ honeydew melon
___ melon baller
___ skewers

Carnival Booths (page 12)
___ tables, benches, or large boxes
___ colorful tablecloths or sheets
___ bright contact paper
___ construction paper
___ paint and paintbrushes
___ balloons and streamers
___ prizes

Face Painting (page 14)
___ face-painting kit

Prize Bags (page 12)
___ white lunch bags
___ ribbon
___ fabric paint and glitter
___ stickers
___ party prizes and candies

Penny Toss (page 13)
___ five small cans
___ wrapping paper or contact paper
___ cardboard or plywood (10" x 13")
___ bright-colored paper
___ pennies

Catch the Bead (page 13)
___ 9-oz plastic cups
___ yarn
___ large round beads
___ permanent markers
___ stickers

Bottle Buddies Knock-Down (page 13)
___ three plastic 2-liter soda bottles
___ three 4" or 5" Styrofoam balls
___ stickers
___ colored electrical tape
___ ribbon
___ rubber balls or beanbags

Stand-up Clowns (page 14)
___ toilet paper tubes
___ colored paper
___ newspaper and white paper towels
___ rubber bands
___ ½" pompoms

Clown Straws (page 14)
___ drinking straws
___ heavy white paper
___ colored paper
___ craft knife

Masks (page 14)
___ face masks
___ feathers and pompoms
___ sequins and glitter
___ stickers

Decorations & Miscellaneous
___ invitations and thank-you cards
___ plates, cups, and utensils
___ tablecloths and napkins
___ balloons, streamers, and confetti
___ camera, film, and music tapes
___ beverages

NOTE: This list does not include common art supplies (e.g., markers, glue, tape, pencils, scissors, hole punch), or cooking utensils.

SOCCER

SMALL PENNANT PATTERN
(for Corner-Kick Gelatin on page 21)

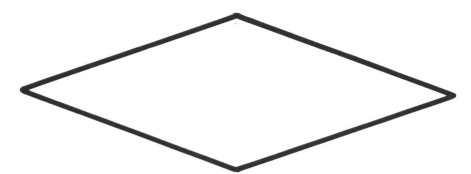

Pennant Directions
1. Trace the pennant patterns on colored construction paper.

2. Cut out the pennants and fold each one in half.

3. Unfold each pennant and place a toothpick or craft stick in the fold. Glue each pennant shut.

LARGE PENNANT PATTERN
(for Soccer Field Cake on page 20)

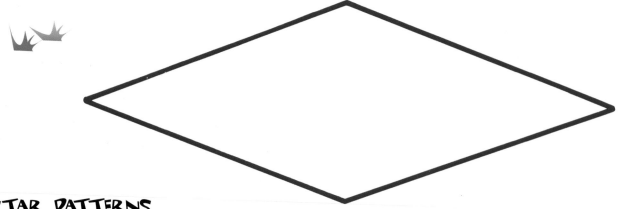

STAR PATTERNS
(page 24)

GETTING STARTED

A great party depends on successful planning. Use this practical guide to help you get ready for the best Soccer Party ever!

One Month Before the Party

___ Decide on day, time, and location.
___ Write a guest list. (Keep the number manageable.)

Two to Three Weeks Before the Party

___ Make a tentative schedule of party activities.
___ Buy (or make) and send out invitations. Include an RSVP.
___ Make a list of decorations, food, and activity supplies.
___ Make or buy party decorations (e.g., banners, streamers, hats).
___ Collect or buy items needed for games and crafts.
___ Buy colorful party table items (e.g., paper plates, cups, utensils, tablecloth, napkins).
___ Buy food items that do not need to be refrigerated.
___ Buy party favors and prizes.
___ Make props for games.
___ Decide on indoor and/or outdoor areas for the games, crafts, foods, and gifts.
___ Select party music (optional).

Week of the Party

___ Finalize party schedule.
___ Call any guests who have not responded.
___ Buy last-minute food and party supplies.
___ Borrow tables, chairs, and other needed items.
___ Prepare foods that can be made ahead of time. (Soccer Field Cake, Sporty Trail Mix, Power Punch, and Corner-Kick Gelatin can be made the day before.)

___ Make cake or order one.
___ Order balloons.
___ Cut out all the craft patterns and prepare a bag or box of materials for each craft.
___ Prepare all games.
___ Check CD or cassette player, video recorder, and/or camera to be sure they're working.

Day of the Party

Four hours before

___ Set the party table.
___ Set up decorations, games, and crafts.
___ Pick up cake (if ordered).
___ Pick up balloons (if ordered).

One to two hours before

___ Complete last-minute foods and drinks.
___ Set out snacks.
___ Make sure your child is dressed for the party and ready to greet guests.
___ Organize music (optional).

As guests arrive

___ Greet guests and make them feel welcome.
___ Have paper and pen available to write down telephone or pager numbers where parents can be reached if needed.

SOCCER FIELD CAKE

Serve this winning cake to your young sports fans!

INGREDIENTS AND SUPPLIES

- cake mix of your choice
- prepared vanilla frosting
- white decorating icing
- green food coloring
- green edible glitter
- 9" x 13" cake pan
- 11" x 15" sheet of cardboard covered with aluminum foil, or a serving platter
- large colored toothpicks or craft sticks
- soccer player figures and two soccer goals
- pennant pattern (page 18)
- construction paper
- permanent marker
- scissors
- glue

DIRECTIONS

1. Mix, bake, and cool cake according to package directions.
2. Remove the cake from its pan and place it on a foil-covered sheet of cardboard or a serving platter.
3. Add green food coloring to the vanilla frosting, and ice the entire cake.
4. Sprinkle green edible glitter on the top of the cake.
5. Using a toothpick, draw the lines of a soccer field on the frosted cake.
6. Using white decorating icing, pipe lines of frosting over the toothpick-drawn lines.
7. Place the soccer players and soccer goals on the cake.
8. Construct three pennants as described on page 18.
9. Write the word *Happy* on the first pennant, *Birthday* on the second pennant, and the birthday child's name on the third pennant. Insert the pennants in sequence along one side of the cake.

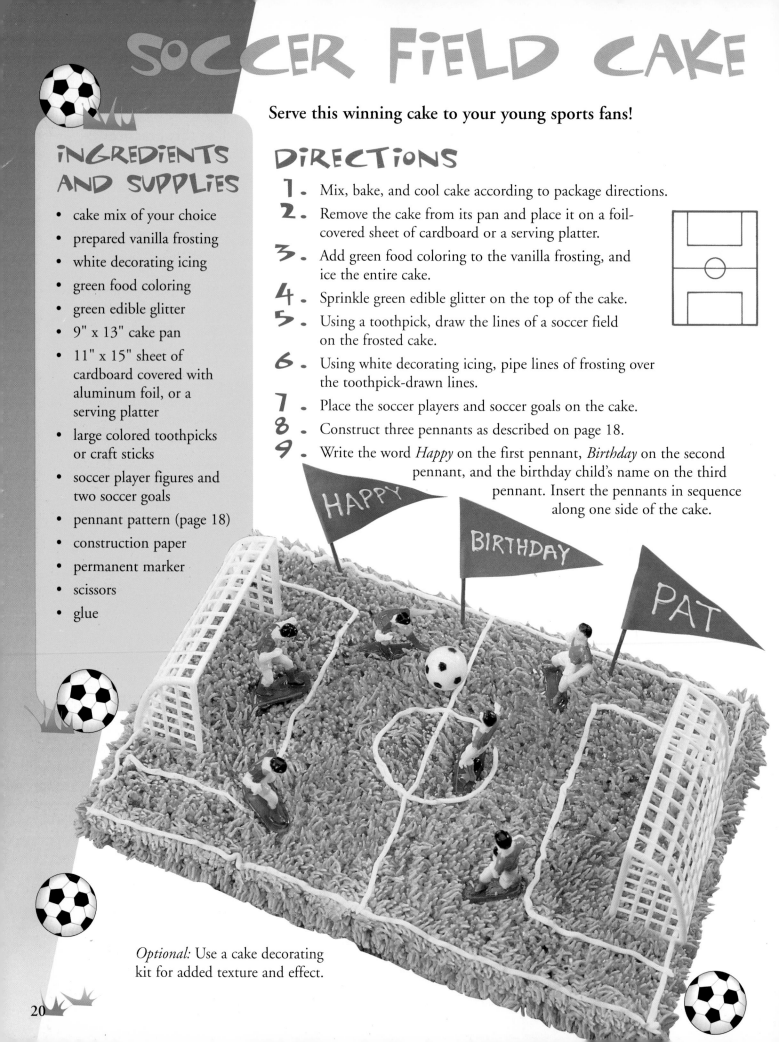

Optional: Use a cake decorating kit for added texture and effect.

PARTY FOODS

Your guests will get a kick out of these delicious party treats!

SOCCER-BALL PIZZA

Ingredients and Supplies (for 12 mini pizzas): 6 English muffins, ¾ cup spaghetti sauce, 1⅓ cups of shredded mozzarella cheese, 5-oz package of sliced pepperoni, shallow baking sheet, plastic soccer figures (washed with soap and hot water)

Directions

1. Split the English muffins in half. Spread spaghetti sauce on top of each half.

2. Sprinkle mozzarella cheese over the sauce and top with pepperoni.

3. Place the muffins on a baking sheet. Bake at 425° for 10 to 12 minutes or until cheese is melted.

4. Top each pizza with a plastic soccer figure.

CORNER-KICK GELATIN

Ingredients and Supplies (for 16 gelatin squares): 6-oz box of fruit-flavored gelatin, two packets of unflavored gelatin, 8" pan, bowl, plate, colored toothpicks (one for each child), measuring cup, knife, small pennant pattern (page 18), construction paper, glue, marker, scissors, stickers (optional)

Directions

1. Pour two cups of water, two packets of unflavored gelatin, and a box of fruit-flavored gelatin into a pan. Stir and heat mixture until all granules are dissolved.

2. Remove from heat and add 2 cups of cold water.

3. Pour into an 8" square dish and refrigerate until firm.

4. Cut into 2" squares and place on a plate.

5. Construct pennants as described on page 18. Write a child's name or a message on each pennant. Insert a pennant into each gelatin square.

FRUIT-O-LICIOUS BOWL

Ingredients and Supplies: large oranges, watermelon, cantaloupe, honeydew melon, or other fruits of choice; melon baller; sharp knife

Directions

1. Cut each orange in half.

2. Carefully cut out the flesh of the orange, leaving the peel to serve as a bowl. Save the orange pieces for the fruit mix.

3. Cut each melon in half and spoon out the seeds. Using a melon baller, scoop out melon balls.

4. Mix the melon balls and orange pieces together and spoon the mixture into each orange half.

SPORTY TRAIL MIX

For a flavorful party snack, mix together 5 cups of cheese puffs, 2 cups of pretzel sticks, 2 cups of Crispix or Corn Chex cereal, and 4 cups of popcorn in a large plastic soccer bowl or other serving bowl.

POWER PUNCH

Combine 3 cups of orange juice and 5 cups of Fierce Melon Gatorade (or fruit punch) in a large pitcher. Chill until ready to serve.

GAMES AND

Score big with these cool games and activities! Prizes, if any, should suit the age range of your guests as well as the theme of the party. Each child should receive several prizes. Consider stickers, pencils, key chains, medallions, chocolate soccer balls, miniature soccer balls, and other theme-related items.

CRAB BALL

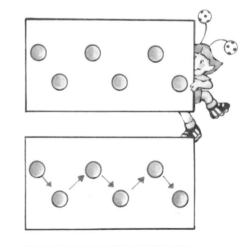

Materials: soccer ball; 4 cones, chairs, or other markers

Directions

1. Mark a large play area in the shape of a square.

2. Choose two or three players to begin the game as "crabs." Have them move to the center of the play area, lie on their backs, and push their bodies off the ground with their hands and feet. The remaining players, the "dribblers," form a line outside the play area.

3. One at a time, players must dribble the ball into the square and try to get the ball past the crabs. Remember, the ball must stay on the ground and be dribbled, not kicked.

4. If a player dribbles the ball out of the square, he or she gets in line to try again. If a crab kicks the ball out of the square, then the dribbler becomes a crab.

5. As more crabs are added, enlarge the boundaries of the square.

6. Continue the game until there is only one player left dribbling the ball. A prize can be awarded to the winning dribbler. Be sure to give the first crabs a chance to be dribblers in future Crab Ball games.

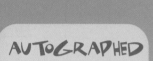

KICK-AND-PASS RELAY

Materials: 2 soccer balls

Directions

1. Divide the children into two teams. Stagger the players in each team, as shown in the top diagram. The children should stand about four or five feet from one another.

2. Place a ball at the feet of the first player in each team.

3. At the signal *Go!*, the first player on each team kicks the ball, passing it to the next player. Players continue kicking and passing the ball until it reaches the last player.

4. When the last player gets the ball, he or she kicks it so that it is passed back down the line.

5. Players continue kicking and passing the ball until it reaches the first player on the team. The first team to complete all passes wins.

ACTIVITIES

SOCCER BLOCKER

This game works best with a group of at least 10 children.

Materials: soccer ball

Directions

1. Players stand in a large circle, with one child in the middle. That child is the "Soccer Blocker."

2. One player standing on the edge of the circle kicks the ball to a child on the other side.

3. The Soccer Blocker tries to stop the ball by intercepting it. If successful, he or she takes a place at the edge of the circle, and the child who kicked the ball that was blocked becomes the new Soccer Blocker.

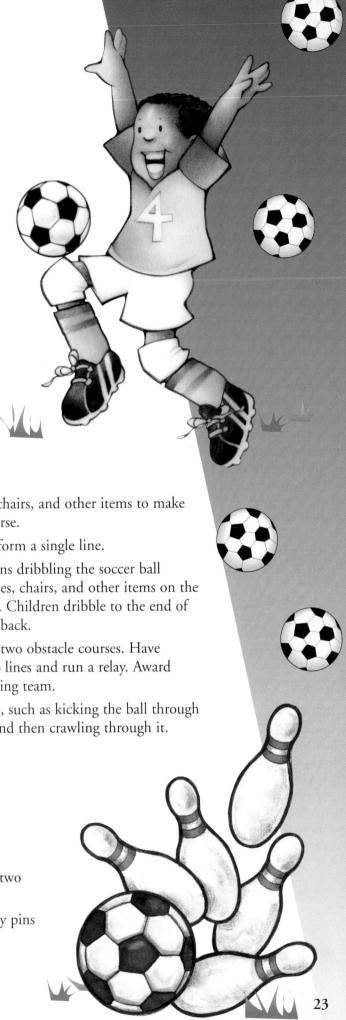

OBSTACLE DRIBBLE

Materials: obstacle course items (e.g., cones, chairs, hoops), soccer ball

Directions

1. Set out cones, chairs, and other items to make an obstacle course.

2. Have children form a single line.

3. Guests take turns dribbling the soccer ball around the cones, chairs, and other items on the obstacle course. Children dribble to the end of the course and back.

Variations: Set up two obstacle courses. Have children form two lines and run a relay. Award prizes to the winning team.

Add silly activities, such as kicking the ball through a cardboard box and then crawling through it.

SOCCER BOWLING

Materials: 5 plastic bowling pins (use 2-liter soda bottles weighted with water if bowling pins are unavailable), soccer ball

Directions

1. Set up bowling pins on the grass or pavement. Line them up in two rows: two pins in the front and three pins in the back.

2. Children take turns kicking the ball and knocking down as many pins as they can.

Variation: Divide the children into two teams. Players take turns knocking down the pins. One point is scored for each pin knocked down. The team with the most points wins.

SOCCER CRAFTS

Your guests will have loads of fun with these party crafts, and also will have some great keepsakes to take home. If you have room, prepare a separate table with a plastic tablecloth for your craft projects and supplies.

PARTY BAGS

Have white party bags, glitter glue, puffy paints, markers, and stickers available for guests as they arrive. Have guests write their name on a bag and decorate it with available materials. Children can fill their bags with treats and prizes throughout the party. Have extra favors on hand to be sure everyone goes home with several items.

PERSONALIZED PENNANTS

Materials: 9" x 12" pieces of felt (1 piece makes 2 pennants), felt scraps, star patterns (page 18) traced and cut from tagboard, pencil, scissors, glue, hole punch, 12" dowels (¼" in diameter), letter stencils (optional)

Directions

1. Cut the piece of felt along its diagonal to make two triangular pennants.

2. With the hole punch, make four holes along the short side of each triangle.

3. Working freehand or using stencils, cut out initials from felt. Glue them onto the pennant. (For younger children, cut out initials beforehand.)

4. Cut out felt shapes freehand or with the help of stencils or star patterns. Glue the shapes on the pennant.

5. Weave a dowel through the holes of the pennant.

SPORTY VISORS

Buy plastic visors at a local craft or party store. Have fabric paints, soccer stickers, sequins, and glue available for children to decorate their visors.

SPORTS CARDS MEMENTOS

Materials: Polaroid camera and film, soccer shirt and soccer ball, 3½" x 5" pieces of card stock (1 for each child), 3" x 4½" pieces of card stock of contrasting color, scissors, glue, markers

Directions

1. Before the party, write a child's name on the top of each piece of 3" x 4½" card stock. At the bottom, write the birthday child's name and the date.

2. Take a photo of each child wearing the soccer shirt and holding the soccer ball.

3. After the photo is developed, trim it to fit onto the 3" x 4½" piece of card stock (approximately 2½" x 3½"). Glue the photo onto the card.

4. Glue the photo and card onto the 3½" x 5" piece of card stock.

Variation: If an instant camera is not available, have photos developed after the party. Make thank-you notes by gluing the sports cards on the front of blank note cards. Write a message inside.

DECORATIONS

Here's a creative game plan to help you set the tone for a super-cool soccer party! Cover the party table with a green tablecloth and use soccer-themed paper plates and cups. Hang black and white balloons in bunches near the table, from the backs of chairs, or from a light above the table. Place streamers on the table or draped from a string hung above the table. Display posters of soccer players around the party room.

Line up two rows of plastic cones to form a path leading to your front door. Tape black and white balloons and sports pennants to the door. Dress up a large stuffed doll in a T-shirt and a pair of shorts, and place a pennant or a toy soccer ball in its hands. Sit the doll in a chair near the front door to greet your guests as they arrive.

SOCCER PARTY SHOPPING LIST

Use this handy checklist to help you plan the items you'll need to buy or gather for your party. Check off items as you get them.

Soccer Field Cake *(page 20)*

___ cake mix
___ prepared vanilla frosting
___ white decorating icing
___ green food coloring
___ edible glitter (green)
___ cake decorating kit (optional)
___ 11" x 15" sheet of cardboard and aluminum foil
___ colored toothpicks or craft sticks
___ construction paper
___ soccer player figures and goals

Soccer-Ball Pizza *(page 21)*

___ English muffins
___ spaghetti sauce
___ shredded mozzarella cheese
___ pepperoni
___ plastic soccer figures

Corner-Kick Gelatin *(page 21)*

___ fruit-flavored gelatin
___ unflavored gelatin
___ colored toothpicks
___ construction paper

Fruit-o-licious Bowl *(page 21)*

___ oranges
___ watermelon, cantaloupe, honeydew melon, or other fruits
___ melon baller

Sporty Trail Mix *(page 21)*

___ cheese puffs
___ pretzel sticks
___ Crispix or Corn Chex cereal
___ popcorn

Power Punch *(page 21)*

___ orange juice
___ Fierce Melon Gatorade or fruit punch

Crab Ball *(page 22)*

___ soccer ball
___ cones, chairs, or other markers

Autographed Soccer Ball *(page 22)*

___ soccer ball
___ permanent markers

Obstacle Dribble *(page 23)*

___ soccer ball
___ cones, chairs, hoops, or other items for obstacle course

Soccer Bowling *(page 23)*

___ soccer ball
___ plastic bowling pins or 2-liter soda bottles

Party Bags *(page 24)*

___ white party bags
___ glitter glue
___ puffy paints
___ stickers

Personalized Pennants *(page 24)*

___ 9" x 12" felt pieces
___ felt scraps
___ tagboard
___ dowels

Sporty Visors *(page 24)*

___ plastic visors
___ fabric paints
___ soccer stickers
___ sequins

Sports Cards Mementos *(page 24)*

___ Polaroid camera and film
___ soccer shirt
___ soccer ball
___ card stock in two contrasting colors

Decorations and Miscellaneous

___ invitations and thank-you notes
___ plates, cups, napkins, tablecloth
___ eating utensils
___ balloons, streamers, confetti
___ party treats and prizes
___ soccer balls
___ camera and film
___ beverages

NOTE: This list does not include common art supplies (e.g., markers, glue, tape, pencils, scissors, hole punch) or cooking utensils.

Dinosaurs

TERRiFic TReaT Holder Pattern

(page 34)

Stand-up Dinosaur Pattern

(page 34)

Dino-Mite T-shirt Pattern

(page 34)

Getting Started

A great party depends on successful planning. Use this handy guide
to help you get ready for the best Dinosaur Party ever!

One Month Before the Party

___ Decide on day, time, and location.
___ Write a guest list. (Keep the number manageable.)
___ Make a tentative schedule of party activities.

Two to Three Weeks Before the Party

___ Buy (or make) and send out invitations.
Include an RSVP.
___ Make a list of decorations, food, and
activity supplies.
___ Make or buy party decorations (e.g., banners,
streamers, hats).
___ Buy items needed for games and crafts.
___ Buy colorful party table items (e.g., paper plates,
cups, utensils, tablecloth, napkins).
___ Buy food items that do not need to be
refrigerated.
___ Buy goody bag treats and prizes.
___ Decide on an area for the games, crafts, and gifts.
___ Select background party music (optional).

Week of the Party

___ Finalize party schedule.
___ Call any guests who have not responded.
___ Buy last-minute foods and party supplies.
___ Borrow tables, chairs, and other needed items.

___ Prepare foods that can be made ahead of time
(e.g., Dino-Mite Dinosaur Cake, Herbivore
Dino-Dip, raw vegetables).
___ Make cake or order one.
___ Order balloons.
___ Cut out craft patterns and prepare a bag of
materials for each craft. Make sample crafts.
___ Prepare plaster of Paris cartons for Fossil Finds.
___ Check CD or cassette player, video recorder, and/or
camera to be sure they're working.

Day of the Party

Four hours before

___ Pick up cake (if ordered).
___ Pick up balloons (if ordered).
___ Set the party table.
___ Set up games, crafts, and decorations.

One to two hours before

___ Organize music (optional).
___ Complete last-minute foods and drinks.
___ Set out munchies.
___ Make sure your child is dressed for the party
and ready to greet guests.

As guests arrive

___ Greet guests and make them feel welcome.
___ Have paper and pen available to write down
telephone or pager numbers where parents
can be reached if needed.

Dinosaur Cake

All of your "cake-a-vores" will love this adorable dinosaur cake. Add a scoop of rocky road ice cream per serving to complete this yummy treat.

Ingredients and Supplies

- cake mix of your choice
- prepared vanilla frosting
- green food coloring
- green sugar sprinkles
- tubes of decorating icing
- craft eye
- two 8" round cake pans
- rocky road ice cream
- mixing bowls, spoons, measuring cup, hand mixer, large knife, cooling racks, toothpicks, serving tray

Directions

1. Bake two cakes in the 8" round pans according to the directions on the cake mix box.

2. Cool the cakes in the pans for 15 minutes. Remove from pans and cool completely on racks.

3. Carefully slice off the rounded tops of each cake to make two flat circles.

4. Cut the cakes into pieces as shown. Arrange the pieces to form a dinosaur shape. Use the remaining pieces of cake to cut triangle-shaped spikes.

5. Secure the spikes to the dinosaur's back with toothpicks.

6. Add green food coloring to the vanilla frosting and ice the entire cake.

7. Add a craft eye and other details using decorating icing.

8. Sprinkle the cake with sugar sprinkles.

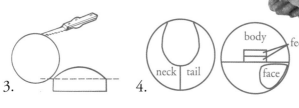

3.   4.

neck | tail   body   feet
               face

Optional: Use a cake decorating kit and a variety of food colorings for added texture and effect.

30

Party Foods

Involve party-going paleontologists in making individual dinosaur pockets for a yummy party treat. Round out the menu with vegetables and dip, frozen pops, cookies, and other munchies kids love.

Individual Dinosaur Pockets

Ingredients and Supplies (makes 8 dinosaurs): 2 tubes of Pillsbury pizza crust, pizza sauce, pocket fillings (e.g., pepperoni, shredded cheese, assorted vegetables), 2 egg whites, raisins or peppercorns, round cookie cutter (approximately 5" diameter), cooking spray or butter, large baking sheet, paper plates, pastry brush, fork, small containers, spoons

Directions

1. Fill small containers with various pocket fillings.
2. Preheat oven to 425°. Grease or spray cookie sheet.
3. Press each tube of dough into a 15" x 11" rectangle.
4. Using a cookie cutter, cut circles from the dough.
5. Place a circle of dough and some dough scraps on each paper plate.
6. Invite guests to spread sauce on the dough to within an inch of the sides and place ingredients of their choice in the middle.
7. Fold each circle of dough in half and seal the edges by pressing them down with a fork.
8. Use the remaining dough for the dinosaur's features. Use egg white to act as a "glue" and to brush the dinosaur's body.
9. Bake at 425° for about 12 minutes or until browned.

More Yummy Foods

For more food fun, make a variety of dinosaur-shaped sandwiches using dinosaur cookie cutters, bread, and kids' favorite fillings.

Children will love decorating dinosaur crackers using colored frosting and candy sprinkles.

Ice Age Pops

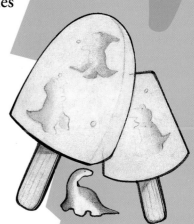

Ingredients and Supplies: candy dinosaurs (gummy dinosaurs), lemonade, ice pop molds

Directions

1. Fill molds with lemonade.
2. Add a few dinosaur candies to each pop and freeze overnight.

Note: If you do not have molds, pour lemonade into small paper cups and cover with plastic wrap. Poke craft sticks through the plastic for handles. Peel off the paper when the pops are frozen.

Herbivore Dino-Dip

Ingredients and Supplies: 2 to 3 ripe avocados, garlic salt, 1 cup mayonnaise, 1 cup sour cream, lemon juice (to taste), corn chips, raw cut vegetables

Directions

1. Mash the avocados in a mixing bowl.
2. Add the garlic salt, mayonnaise, sour cream, and lemon juice, and mix well.
3. Serve this tasty dip with chips and vegetables.

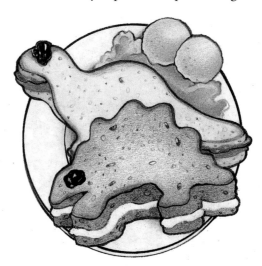

GAMES and

Introduce these hilarious games and activities, then have your camera ready to record the fun! Prizes, if any, should suit the age of your guests as well as the theme. Consider stickers, small plastic dinosaurs, candies, and other dinosaur-related items. Be sure each child receives several prizes.

CARNIVORES VS. HERBIVORES

Materials: dinosaur stickers, whistle

Directions

1. Separate the guests into two teams, the Carnivores and the Herbivores.
2. Give each Carnivore a small sheet of dinosaur stickers. When you blow the whistle, the Carnivores chase the Herbivores. A Herbivore is "caught" when a Carnivore places a sticker on his or her back. The Herbivore must "freeze" until another Herbivore releases him or her by removing the sticker. Play until the Carnivores run out of stickers.
3. Distribute stickers to the Herbivores and repeat the game. The Herbivores can now seek revenge on the Carnivores!

Dinosaur Gossip

Materials: paper, pencil

Directions

1. Before the party, write short, funny sentences that include the names of dinosaurs.
2. Invite partygoers to sit in a circle.
3. Choose one of the sentences and whisper it only once to the player sitting on your right.
4. The player then must whisper what he or she thinks was said to the person on his or her right. This is repeated around the circle. The last person says aloud what he or she heard. Read the original sentence. Don't be surprised when the sentence ends up sounding different!

Hatch-The-Dinosaur-Eggs Relay

Materials: balloons, small plastic dinosaurs or stickers, masking tape or other floor marker

Directions

1. Before the party, carefully place small plastic dinosaurs or dinosaur stickers inside the balloons. Then blow them up and tie them off. Blow up lots of balloons (kids will want to play this game more than once).
2. Divide the group into two equal teams and encourage children to name their teams with favorite dinosaur names.
3. Place the balloons on the floor or ground at one end of the play area. Line up the two teams behind a marker at the other end of the play area. If playing outdoors, tie string to the balloons and anchor them to keep them from blowing away.
4. When a signal is given, the first person on each team runs to the balloons and "hatches" one by sitting or stomping on it. No hands allowed! The player retrieves the dinosaur or sticker, runs back to the team, and tags the next person, who repeats the "egg hatching."
5. The first team to complete the "hatching" wins the game.

Hint: To make the game more challenging, add a mini-obstacle course on the way to the balloons. For example, add cardboard boxes to crawl through or buckets to jump over.

The Tyrann teases ti Titanosaur tickl tickle

A Triceratops' teeth chew tough treats

Activities

Fossil Finds

Materials: ½-pint milk cartons, small plastic dinosaurs, plaster of Paris, simple tools (e.g., dull knives, hammers, toothbrushes)

Directions

1. Place a plastic dinosaur in each milk carton and fill with plaster of Paris. Let harden overnight.
2. At the party, provide guests with simple tools to uncover their dinosaur "fossils"!

Tyrannosaurus Terrariums

Materials: small glass jars with lids or disposable clear plastic containers, potting soil, multicolored aquarium gravel, bedding plants or succulents, small plastic dinosaurs, water

Directions

1. Fill jar about ¼ or ⅓ full with potting soil.
2. Place a small plant in the soil. Sprinkle with aquarium gravel.
3. Place a plastic dinosaur near the plant. Add about a teaspoon of water and place the lid on the jar.

Prehistoric Playtime

Set up a prehistoric play area that guests go to as they arrive and return to between activities. Children will love creating new scenes and acting out dinosaur encounters.

Materials: sandbox or wading pool, sand, plastic toy dinosaurs of all shapes and sizes, rocks, sand buckets, shovels, spoons, leaves and twigs, green tissue paper, paper-towel tubes, boiled and bleached chicken leg bones or plastic bones, glue

Directions

1. Fill a sandbox or wading pool with slightly damp sand. Place toy dinosaurs, rocks, buckets, shovels, spoons, leaves, and twigs on the sand.
2. Make palm trees by gluing green tissue pieces to the tops of paper towel tubes and stand them up in the sand.
3. Bury bones and invite party-going paleontologists to dig for "fossils."

Dinosaur Crafts

Your guests not only will have loads of fun with these party crafts, but also will have some great keepsakes to take home! If you have room, prepare a separate table with a plastic tablecloth for your craft projects and supplies.

Terrific Treat Holders

Older partygoers can make the treat holders themselves. For younger children, complete steps 1–4 beforehand.

Materials (for one treat holder): 2 white paper plates, piece of green tagboard, 2 large wiggly eyes, 12" piece of green yarn, green tempera paint and small paint sponges (or green dot paint), dinosaur pattern (page 28), party favors (e.g., candy, dinosaur stickers, small plastic dinosaurs), markers, scissors, glue, pencil, stapler

Directions

1. Enlarge and trace the dinosaur pattern pieces on green tagboard and cut them out.
2. Place one plate on the table, faceup. Glue on dinosaur pattern pieces and yarn. Place the remaining paper plate on top of the first, bottom side up.
3. Staple the paper plates together, leaving the top open. Write a guest's name on the plate.
4. Use paint sponges to decorate the front and back of the dinosaur. When dry, glue on wiggly eyes.
5. Fill treat holders with party favors.

Stand-Up Dinosaurs

Materials: brightly colored tagboard, dinosaur pattern (page 28), colored plastic clothespins, wiggly eyes, collage materials (e.g., macaroni, sequins, buttons, foam paper), glitter glue, scissors

Complete step 1 beforehand.

Directions

1. Cut out colorful dinosaurs using tagboard and the dinosaur pattern.

2. Decorate the dinosaur with wiggly eyes and collage materials.
3. Glue on clothespins for dinosaur legs.

Dino-Mite T-shirts

Materials: white T-shirts, self-adhesive shelf paper, fabric paint, paper plates, small sponges, newspaper, dinosaur pattern (page 28), scissors or craft knife

Directions

1. Cut shelf paper into 6" to 7" squares—one to three cutouts per guest.
2. Draw or trace dinosaurs on the paper pieces.
3. Use sharp scissors or a craft knife to cut dinosaur shapes from the squares, creating stencils.
4. Lay the T-shirts flat and insert a thick layer of newspaper inside each.
5. Peel the backs from the shelf-paper stencils and place the dinosaur stencils on each shirt.
6. Pour fabric paint on paper plates. Dampen and wring out sponges.
7. Dip a sponge in fabric paint and blot the cutout dinosaur.
8. Remove the stencils carefully when paint has set (about 15 minutes). Allow paint to dry thoroughly before wearing T-shirt.

Decorations

Choose dinosaur plates, cups, and utensils to enhance the party's theme. Add color and excitement to your party table with balloons, streamers, and confetti. Hang balloons in bunches near the table, from the backs of chairs, or from a light above the table. For a festive effect, place streamers on the table or drape them from a light above the table. Add dinosaur props, such as inflatable dinosaurs and plastic figurines.

To welcome your guests, hang balloons and streamers on the mailbox and the front door. Cut out dinosaur footprints and tape them in a trail to the party entrance.

Dinosaur Party Shopping List

Use this handy checklist to help you plan the items you'll need to buy or gather for your party. Check off items as you get them.

Dinosaur Cake (page 30)

____ cake mix
____ vanilla frosting
____ green food coloring
____ green sugar sprinkles
____ tubes of decorating icing
____ rocky road ice cream
____ toothpicks

Individual Dinosaur Pockets (page 31)

____ 2 tubes of Pillsbury pizza crust
____ pizza sauce
____ pocket fillings (e.g., shredded cheese, pepperoni, assorted vegetables)
____ eggs
____ raisins or peppercorns
____ cooking spray or butter
____ round cookie cutter (approximately 5" diameter)

Ice Age Pops (page 31)

____ gummy dinosaurs
____ lemonade
____ ice pop molds or paper cups, plastic wrap, and craft sticks

Herbivore Dino-Dip (page 31)

____ 2 to 3 ripe avocados
____ garlic salt
____ mayonnaise
____ sour cream
____ lemon juice
____ corn chips
____ raw cut vegetables

Carnivores vs. Herbivores (page 32)

____ dinosaur stickers
____ whistle

Hatch-the-Dinosaur-Eggs Relay (page 32)

____ balloons
____ small plastic dinosaurs or stickers

Fossil Finds (page 33)

____ milk cartons (½ pint)
____ plastic dinosaurs
____ plaster of Paris
____ small tools (e.g., hammers, toothbrushes, dull knives)

Tyrannosaurus Terrariums (page 33)

____ small glass jars with lids or disposable clear plastic containers
____ potting soil
____ multicolored aquarium gravel
____ small plants, succulents, or ivy
____ small plastic dinosaurs

Prehistoric Playtime (page 33)

____ sandbox or wading pool
____ sand
____ plastic toy dinosaurs of all shapes and sizes
____ sand buckets, shovels, spoons
____ leaves and twigs
____ green tissue paper
____ paper towel tubes
____ clean chicken leg bones or plastic bones

Terrific Treat Holders (page 34)

____ white paper plates
____ green tagboard
____ wiggly eyes
____ green yarn
____ green tempera paint and small sponges, or green dot paint
____ party favors (dinosaur stickers, pencils and erasers, little dinosaur books, gummy dinosaur candy, and other dinosaur-related goodies)

Stand-up Dinosaurs (page 34)

____ tagboard
____ clothespins (plastic colored)
____ wiggly eyes
____ collage materials (e.g., macaroni, sequins, buttons, stickers, foam paper)
____ glitter glue

Dino-mite T-shirts (page 34)

____ white T-shirts
____ self-adhesive shelf paper
____ fabric paint
____ paper plates
____ small sponges
____ newspaper
____ large dinosaur cookie cutter or dinosaur pattern (page 28)
____ craft knife (or scissors)

Decorations and Miscellaneous

____ invitations and thank-you notes
____ plates, cups, and napkins
____ utensils
____ tablecloth
____ balloons, streamers, and confetti
____ prizes or guest gifts
____ camera and film
____ beverages
____ music

NOTE: This list does not include common art supplies (e.g., markers, glue, tape, pencils, scissors, hole punch), cooking utensils (e.g., bowls, spoons, measuring cups), or supplies for More Yummy Foods (page 31).

Star Light, Star Bright Cake

Light up the night with a beautiful, sparkling star cake. Add a scoop of midnight fudge ice cream to top off this yummy treat.

Ingredients and Supplies

- cake mix of your choice
- prepared vanilla frosting
- yellow sugar sprinkles
- tubes of decorating icing or gel
- fudge ice cream
- star pattern (page 38)
- two 8" round cake pans
- mixing bowls
- spoons
- hand mixer
- cooling rack
- cake stand or large plate

Directions *(serves 6)*

1. Bake the cake in two round pans according to directions on the box.

2. Cool the cakes in their pans for 15 minutes. Remove cakes from the pans and cool completely on a rack.

3. Place the cakes in the freezer for 30 minutes so they will be easier to cut and frost.

4. Cut the cakes into a star by carefully placing the star pattern on top of each cake and cutting around it.

5. Frost the top of each cake with icing.

6. Place one cake on top of the other to form a two-layer cake. Frost the sides of the cake.

7. Sprinkle the top with yellow sugar sprinkles. Add decorations and a message using decorating gel or icing.

8. Display the star cake on a cake tray or large plate.

More Fun

Save the extra cake pieces for the night of the party. Allow each guest to frost and decorate a piece.

Party Foods

Pizza, giant submarine sandwiches, a taco bar, and the recipes below are all fun foods for sleepovers! Remember to round out the dinner by setting out trays of vegetables and dip, fresh fruit, and beverages.

Fun Friends in Sleeping Bags

Ingredients and Supplies (makes 8 "sleeping bags"):
one 8-oz can of refrigerated crescent dinner rolls, 2 hot dogs,
catsup, mustard, knife, cookie sheet

Directions

1. Preheat oven to 375°.

2. Separate dough into four rectangles and smooth out the diagonal perforations.

3. Cut each rectangle lengthwise into two strips to make eight 6" x 2" rectangles.

4. Cut the hot dogs in half. Cut each half in half lengthwise.

5. Place a hot dog slice on one end of each rectangle.

6. Fold the extra dough over the hot dog, stretching it slightly so the dough covers about half of the meat. Press the edges together to seal.

7. Place on an ungreased cookie sheet and bake for 11 to 15 minutes or until golden brown.

8. Make a face on each hot dog using catsup or mustard.

Overnight French Toast

Ingredients and Supplies (makes 8 to 12 servings): two baking pans, 9
eggs, 1½ cups half and half, 1½ cups milk, ⅓ cup sugar, ½ tsp cinnamon,
2 tsp vanilla, 1 loaf French bread cut into 16 to 24 slices, syrup, powdered
sugar, cooking spray or butter, strawberries (optional)

Directions

1. Grease the baking pans.

2. In a large bowl, mix eggs, half and half, milk, sugar, cinnamon, and vanilla until well-blended.

3. Arrange bread slices in greased pans.

4. Pour egg mixture over bread, lifting bread until mixture is completely absorbed. Sprinkle with additional cinnamon.

5. Cover with foil and refrigerate.

6. The next morning, bake at 450° for 15 minutes or until golden brown. Serve with warm syrup, powdered sugar, and strawberries.

More Yummy Ideas

Slumber party s'mores can be a fun nighttime treat! Just sandwich chocolate pieces and miniature marshmallows between two graham crackers and microwave on high for about 20 seconds.

Help children prepare individual snack bags to satisfy midnight cravings. Have some yummy ingredients (e.g., popcorn, raisins, granola, nuts, candy pieces, butterscotch chips, pretzels, miniature marshmallows, Cheerios) available for guests to scoop into sandwich-size resealable plastic bags.

Slumber Party

Delight your guests with these fun craft ideas! If you have room, prepare a separate table with a plastic tablecloth for your craft projects and supplies.

Glamour Bags

Materials: black or brown lunch bags, craft sticks or plastic spoons, hole punch, colorful ribbon, star-shaped craft sponges, gold or yellow tempera paint, gold or white glitter, paper plates, water, markers, glamour bag party favors, such as toiletries (e.g., toothbrushes, shampoo samples, soap, lotion), nail polish, and hair accessories

Directions

1. Label each bag with guest's name.

2. Pour paint into paper plates. Add glitter and mix with a craft stick or plastic spoon.

3. Dampen sponges and wring out excess moisture.

4. Lay bags flat. Print stars on the bags by dipping sponges into the paint and pressing lightly on the bag.

5. When the paint dries, fold over the top of each bag and punch two holes through all layers. Pull the ends of the ribbon through the holes and tie a bow in front.

6. Allow time during the party for girls to dig into their bags and use the nail polish, hair accessories, and toiletries.

Picture Frames

Materials: posterboard or cardboard cut into 4" squares, 4" craft sticks (or tongue depressors), collage materials (e.g., stickers, buttons, sequins, small seashells), rickrack or yarn, instant camera and film, glue, tape, scissors

Directions

1. Place two sticks opposite each other on a cardboard square and glue in place.

2. Glue two more craft sticks on frame.

3. Decorate the frame with collage materials.

4. Glue a piece of rickrack or yarn to the back for a hanger.

5. Take instant photos of partygoers and trim the edges.

6. Slide pictures into frames. Secure with tape.

Options: If you do not have an instant camera, send photo later or give each guest a disposable camera to take home.

Creative Kits

Check out the arts and crafts section of your favorite store. There are great kits available (e.g., friendship bracelets, picture making) that your guests will enjoy.

Crafts

Making Memories

Materials: letter-size envelopes (5 to 6 per child),
hole punch, scissors, yarn or ribbon, construction paper, stickers,
foam paper, lined writing paper

Directions

1. Cut off the triangle top of each envelope to
   make a pocket.

2. Cut a cover the size of the envelope from
   construction paper.

3. Hole-punch the cover and inside pocket pages
   on the left side and tie them together with yarn.

4. Fold and crease each page a half inch from the left
   edge to make it easier to turn.

5. Decorate the cover with stickers and colorful paper shapes.

6. Cut pieces of lined paper and glue to the pages.

7. Use the journal as a diary or to record fun times (like the slumber party!).
   Place mementos (e.g., photos, ticket stubs) in the pockets.

Skidproof Slipper Socks

Materials: washed and dried cotton socks (colored or white), cardboard,
pens or markers, scissors, several colors of nontoxic fabric puffy paint

Note: Do not use fabric softener when washing socks.

Directions

1. Trace each guest's feet on pieces of cardboard.
   Cut out patterns. (Older kids can trace each other's feet.)

2. Have children place a cardboard "foot" inside each sock so that
   the bottom is stretched out and flat.

3. Draw a repeated pattern or simple designs on the bottoms of the socks
   using pens or markers. Trace over the designs with puffy paint. Allow to dry overnight.

Personalized Pillowcases

Materials: white prewashed pillowcases, fabric markers,
cardboard or newspaper, pencils

Directions

1. Lay pillowcase flat. Place cardboard or folded newspaper inside the
   pillowcase to prevent markers from bleeding.

2. Have each guest write her name in pencil on the pillowcase. Add a design
   if desired. Trace the name and design with fabric markers.

3. Exchange pillowcases with other guests. Have them sign their names on the
   pillowcase and add drawings or designs.

Games and Activities

Introduce these hilarious games and activities to partygoers, and have your camera ready to record the fun!

Funny Fortunes

Materials: paper, pencils, clipboards or other firm writing surfaces

Directions

1. In advance, duplicate a fill-in-the-blank list for each guest. Include the following prompts: *name, job, place, boy's name, number, color, another color, fun place to go, game.* With the help of the birthday child, make a few sample stories. For example: *Megan is a mountain climber living in Hawaii. She is married to Jason and they have 53 children with purple hair and pink eyes. They all like to go to the bowling alley and play hide-and-seek.*

2. Have the guests sit on the floor in a circle. Explain the game and read a sample story.

3. Distribute copies of the list, pencils, and writing surfaces.

4. Each guest writes her name first, then passes the paper to the person on the left. That person fills in the next blank. Continue passing the papers until all the blanks are filled. Encourage kids to come up with unusual, funny, or silly answers. Have guests take turns reading the answers on the sheets.

Suitcase Relay

Materials: two small suitcases or duffel bags, each filled with large-size items such as pajamas, robe, slippers, shower cap, and undergarments

Directions

1. Divide players into two teams. Give the first player on each team a suitcase.

2. When you say *Go!*, the player opens the suitcase, puts the clothes on over her pajamas, runs to a designated spot with the suitcase, takes off the clothes, puts them back in the suitcase, runs back to the starting place, and hands the suitcase to the next team member.

3. Continue until all players have had a turn.

Balloon Volleyball

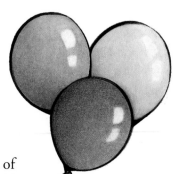

Materials: balloons, jump rope or clothesline

Directions

1. Clear a playing area of furniture and breakables.

2. Blow up several balloons and tie them off. Place a rope across the middle of the playing area to serve as a net. Lay rope on floor, or tie rope to two chairs.

3. Divide the guests into two teams. Have them swat a balloon back and forth over the rope. A team scores a point when the balloon hits the floor on the opponent's side.

Option: For an extra challenge, play the game with two or three balloons.

To welcome your guests, hang balloons and streamers on the mailbox and on the front door.

Decorations

Choose plates, cups, and utensils that enhance your slumber party theme. Add color and excitement to your party table with balloons, streamers, a tablecloth, and confetti. Hang balloons in bunches near the table, from the backs of chairs, or from a light above the table. Place streamers on the table or from a string hung above the table.

Slumber Party Shopping List

Use this handy checklist to help you plan the items you'll need to buy or gather for your party. Check off items as you get them.

Star Light, Star Bright Cake *(page 40)*
____ cake mix
____ prepared vanilla frosting
____ yellow sugar sprinkles
____ decorating gel or icing
____ fudge ice cream

Fun Friends in Sleeping Bags *(page 41)*
____ refrigerated crescent dinner rolls
____ hot dogs
____ catsup and mustard

Overnight French Toast *(page 41)*
____ eggs
____ half and half
____ milk
____ sugar
____ cinnamon
____ vanilla
____ French bread
____ cooking spray or butter
____ syrup
____ powdered sugar
____ strawberries (optional)

S'mores *(page 41)*
____ graham crackers
____ miniature marshmallows
____ milk chocolate bars

Snack Bags *(page 41)*
____ sandwich-size resealable plastic bags
____ any combination of popcorn, raisins, granola, nuts, candy pieces, butterscotch chips, pretzels, miniature marshmallows, Cheerios, and other trail mix ingredients

Glamour Bags *(page 42)*
____ black or brown lunch bags
____ craft sticks or plastic spoons
____ colorful ribbon
____ star-shaped craft sponges
____ gold or yellow tempera paint
____ gold or white glitter
____ sample-size of toiletries, nail polish, and hair accessories

Picture Frames *(page 42)*
____ posterboard or cardboard
____ 4" craft sticks
____ stickers
____ buttons
____ sequins
____ small seashells
____ rickrack or yarn
____ other collage materials of choice
____ instant camera and film

Making Memories *(page 43)*
____ letter-size envelopes (5 to 6 per child)
____ yarn or ribbon
____ construction paper
____ stickers
____ foam paper
____ lined writing paper

Skidproof Slipper Socks *(page 43)*
____ cotton socks
____ cardboard
____ fabric puffy paints

Personalized Pillowcases *(page 43)*
____ white pillowcases
____ fabric markers

Suitcase Relay *(page 44)*
____ 2 small suitcases or duffel bags

Balloon Volleyball *(page 44)*
____ balloons
____ jump rope or clothesline

Decorations and Miscellaneous
____ invitations and thank-you notes
____ plates, cups, napkins
____ eating utensils
____ tablecloths
____ balloons, streamers, confetti
____ music and/or video
____ camera and film
____ beverages

NOTE: This list does not include common art supplies (e.g., markers, glue, tape, pencils, scissors, hole punch), or cooking utensils.

46

Under the Sea

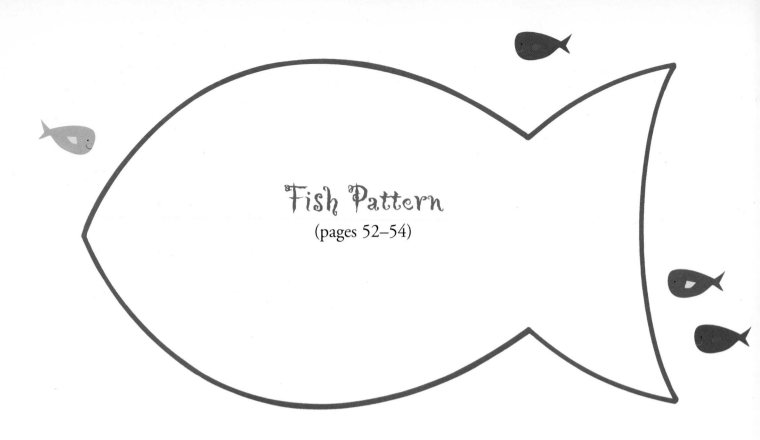

Fish Pattern
(pages 52–54)

Sea Horse Pattern
(page 54)

Whale Tail Pattern
(page 53)

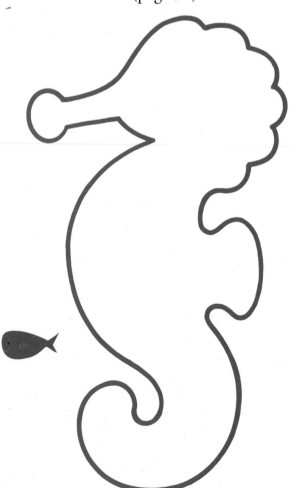

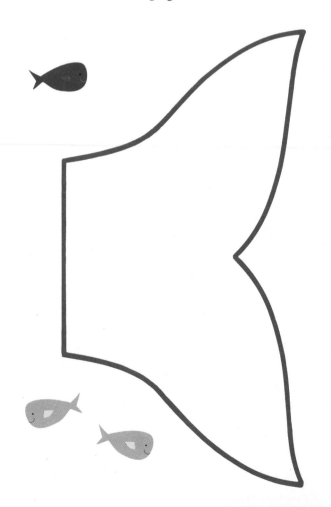

Getting Started

A great party depends on successful planning. Use this handy guide to help you get ready for the best Under-the-Sea Party ever!

One Month Before the Party

___ Decide on day, time, and location.

___ Write a guest list. (Keep the number manageable.)

Two to Three Weeks Before the Party

___ Make a tentative schedule of party activities.

___ Buy or make the invitations.

___ Send out the invitations. Include an RSVP.

___ Make a list of decorations, food, and activity supplies.

___ Make or buy party decorations (e.g., banners, streamers, hats).

___ Buy items needed for games and crafts.

___ Buy colorful party table items (e.g., paper plates, cups, utensils, tablecloth, napkins).

___ Buy food items that do not need to be refrigerated.

___ Buy party favors.

___ Make props and items for games.

___ Select party music (optional).

___ Decide on an area for the games, crafts, and gifts.

Week of the Party

___ Finalize party schedule.

___ Call any guests who have not responded.

___ Buy last-minute foods and party supplies.

___ Borrow tables, chairs, and other needed items.

___ Prepare foods that can be made ahead of time (e.g., Fantasy Fish Cake, Goldfish Party Mix, and Gelatin Sea).

___ Check CD or cassette player, video recorder and/or camera to be sure they're working.

___ Make cake or order one.

___ Order balloons.

___ Cut out craft patterns and prepare a bag of materials for each craft.

___ Prepare all games.

Day of the Party

Four hours before

___ Set the party table.

___ Set up decorations, games, and crafts.

___ Pick up cake (if ordered).

___ Pick up balloons (if ordered).

One to two hours before

___ Organize music (optional).

___ Complete last-minute foods and drinks.

___ Set out snacks.

___ Make sure your child is dressed for the party and ready to greet guests.

As guests arrive

___ Greet guests and make them feel welcome.

___ Have paper and pen available to write down telephone or pager numbers where parents can be reached if needed.

Fantasy Fish Cake

Delight party guests with this surprise "catch of the day"!

Ingredients and Supplies

- cake mix of your choice
- prepared vanilla frosting
- gummy candy rings
- chocolate malt ball, gumball, or chocolate chip
- candy sprinkles
- two 8" round cake pans
- large cookie sheet, thick cardboard, or other serving surface
- aluminum foil
- frosting knife
- food coloring and three containers (optional)

Directions

1. Prepare the cake mix as directed on the box, and bake in two round pans.
2. Cool the cakes in the pans for 15 minutes before removing to cool completely.
3. Cut one of the round cakes into the shape of a tail and two side fins.
4. Cover a serving surface with aluminum foil.
5. Arrange the tail, fins, and body on the surface to form the fish.
6. Frost the cake.
7. Cut gummy candies into thirds. Arrange the pieces over the fish's body to simulate scales.
8. Add a malt ball, gumball, or chocolate chip for the fish's eye and an uncut gummy ring for the mouth.
9. Decorate the tail and fins with candy sprinkles.

Hint: Divide frosting into two or three containers and add different food colorings to use for the body, tail, and fins.

Party Foods

Treat your party guests to a feast of ocean-related goodies!

Fish and Chips

Ingredients and Supplies: *package of frozen fish sticks, package of frozen French fries, catsup, shredded lettuce, shallow baking sheets, deep serving bowl, small paper fish, tape, platter*

Directions

1. Lay the fish and French fries on separate baking sheets, and prepare them as directed on the packages.

2. Tape paper fish around the outside of a deep serving bowl and fill bowl with French fries.

3. Place "seaweed" (shredded lettuce) on a platter and arrange the fish sticks on top. Serve with catsup.

Goldfish Party Mix

Ingredients and Supplies: *3 cups goldfish crackers, 3 cups Chex cereal, 1 cup pretzel sticks, 1 cup peanuts, ½ cup melted margarine, 4 tbsp grated parmesan cheese, large bowl, spoon, microwavable baking dish*

Directions

1. Mix the goldfish crackers, Chex cereal, pretzel sticks, and peanuts in a large bowl. Pour melted margarine over the top and mix well.

2. Place the mixture in a baking dish. Microwave uncovered on high for two minutes.

3. Sprinkle grated parmesan cheese over the mixture. Stir well.

4. Microwave on high for three more minutes. Stir once halfway through cooking time.

5. Let stand for five minutes or until crispy.

Gelatin Sea

Ingredients and Supplies: *two 15-oz cans of fruit cocktail (or one 30-oz can), one 6-oz package of powdered blue gelatin, clear glass serving bowl*

Directions

1. Cover the bottom of a large, clear serving bowl with drained fruit cocktail.

2. Make gelatin according to the directions on the package.

3. Slowly pour the gelatin over the fruit and place uncovered in the refrigerator to chill.

4. Once the gelatin has set, cover bowl with plastic wrap and keep refrigerated until ready to serve.

More Fishy Food Ideas

Use star- or fish-shaped cookie cutters and a variety of fillings to create fun, kid-size sandwiches.

Apply colorful fish stickers or confetti to clear plastic cups. Fill with blue powdered drink mix so that when children hold the cups up to the light, they will see the fish in a glimmering "ocean"!

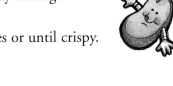

Games and

Dive into a sea of fun with these cool games and activities! Prizes, if any, should suit the age range of your guests as well as the theme of the party. Each child should receive several prizes. Consider stickers, pencils, candies, shells, small plastic sea creatures, and other novelty items.

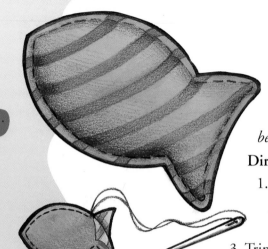

Beanbag Fish Toss

Make some beanbag fish and let children test their throwing skills! Prepare the beanbags ahead of time.

Materials: 12" x 18" piece of lightweight fabric (for three fish), fish pattern (page 48), straight pins, scissors, needle, thread, dried beans, 3 or 4 buckets or boxes, candies and/or small prizes

Directions (for one fish)

1. Use the fish pattern to cut two fish shapes per beanbag.
2. Pin the shapes right sides together. Hand- or machine-stitch ¼" from the edge, leaving a 2" opening at the tail.
3. Trim the material around the seam to reduce the bulk of the fabric.
4. Turn the fish right side out and fill the fish with dried beans. (Do not overstuff.)
5. Fold down the edges of the opening ¼" and sew shut. Topstitch ⅛" from the outer edge if you wish.

Playing the Game

Place candies or small prizes in three or four pails. Place the pails against a wall. Invite children to take turns throwing the fish into a pail. Allow children to choose a prize from whatever bucket the fish land in. (Be sure every child wins a prize.)

Shark Chase

Materials: five or more hula hoops (or carpet squares)

Directions

1. Have the children spread out on one side of the playing area, and tell them they are fish.
2. Scatter the hula hoops or carpet squares around the opposite side of the playing area; the hoops are the fish's "homes."
3. Select one child to be the shark, and have that child stand between the "fish" and their "homes."
4. When the "shark" calls *Shark!,* he or she runs after the "fish" and tries to tag as many as possible. The fish must reach home (step on a carpet square or inside a hula hoop) to be safe from the shark.
5. Any child who is tagged becomes a shark for the next round and also tags remaining fish.
6. For each round, take away one hula hoop until only one hoop is left. Keep playing until all the fish are caught.

Activities

Magnetic Fishing

Prepare the fishing pole, paper fish, and numbered prizes ahead of time.

Materials: 18" stick or dowel, 30" of string, ring or horseshoe magnet, heavy card stock in different colors, paper clips (one for each fish), fish pattern (page 48), scissors, felt markers, prizes (one per fish), wrapping paper or plastic bags for prizes, container for prizes, wading pool or large box

Directions

1. Tie one end of the string to the stick. Tie the other end to the magnet.

2. Trace the fish pattern onto colored card stock. Cut out the fish. Make at least two more fish than the number of children attending the party.

3. Draw facial features on the front side of each fish. Secure a paper clip to the tail. Write a number on the back of each fish.

4. Wrap the prizes in paper or place them in individual plastic bags. Number the prizes to match the numbers on the fish. Place the prizes in a container. Every child wins a surprise in this game!

Playing the Game

Scatter the fish in an empty wading pool or a large shallow box. Let children take turns fishing with the pole. The numbers on the fish they catch determine their prizes.

Pin the Tail on the Whale

Materials: white posterboard or foam board (approximately 22" x 28"), 18" x 24" sheet of gray construction paper, 9" x 12" sheets of gray construction paper (each sheet makes five tails), tail pattern (page 48), pencil, scissors, felt marker, ruler, glue, masking tape, blindfold

Whale Board and Tails

Draw a large whale on the larger-size gray paper, leaving out the tail and, instead, tapering the end of its body to a width of two inches. Cut out the whale and glue it to the board. Draw blue waves around the whale. Tape the board to a wall. On the 9" x 12" gray paper, use the tail pattern to cut out one tail per child. Number the tails.

Playing the Game

1. Have children stand several feet away from the whale. Attach a piece of masking tape, rolled to expose the sticky side, to the back of each numbered tail.

2. Blindfold children one at a time and give him or her a tail. Have each child walk toward the whale and attach the tail to the board. Undo the blindfold so the child can see where he or she placed the tail.

3. The child whose tail is closest to where the whale's tail should be wins the game.

Under-the-Sea Party Shopping List

Use this handy checklist to help you plan the items you'll need to buy or gather for your party. Check off items as you get them.

Fantasy Fish Cake *(page 50)*
___ cake mix
___ food coloring (optional)
___ gummy candy rings
___ chocolate malt ball, gumball, or chocolate chip
___ candy sprinkles
___ prepared vanilla frosting
___ aluminum foil

Fish and Chips *(page 51)*
___ frozen fish sticks
___ frozen French fries
___ shredded lettuce
___ paper for fish cutouts
___ catsup

Gelatin Sea *(page 51)*
___ two 15-oz cans of fruit cocktail
___ 6-oz package of powdered blue gelatin

Goldfish Party Mix *(page 51)*
___ goldfish crackers
___ Chex cereal
___ pretzel sticks
___ peanuts
___ margarine
___ grated parmesan cheese

Beanbag Fish Toss *(page 52)*
___ 12" x 18" lightweight fabric (makes three fish)
___ dried beans
___ buckets or boxes
___ candies or small prizes

Shark Chase *(page 52)*
___ hula hoops or carpet squares

Magnetic Fishing *(page 53)*
___ 18" stick or dowel
___ string
___ ring or horseshoe magnet
___ heavy card stock

___ paper clips
___ prizes
___ wrapping paper or plastic bags
___ wading pool or large box

Pin the Tail on the Whale *(page 53)*
___ white posterboard or foam board (22" x 28")
___ 18" x 24" sheet of gray construction paper
___ 9" x 12" sheets of gray construction paper
___ blindfold

Octopus Goody Bags *(page 54)*
___ blue or white paper bags
___ pipe cleaners
___ colored construction paper
___ crepe-paper streamers
___ white and black paper

Creature Magnets *(page 54)*
___ 12" x 18" sheets of crafting foam
___ sequins, rickrack, beads, etc.
___ craft eyes
___ magnetic tape

Seascape Gel Bags *(page 54)*
___ resealable plastic bags
___ blue hair gel
___ foam paper
___ fish-shaped confetti
___ colored beads
___ small seashells
___ clear packing tape
___ glitter

Decorations and Miscellaneous
___ invitations and thank-you notes
___ plates, cups, napkins, and tablecloths
___ utensils
___ balloons, streamers, and confetti
___ party prizes
___ camera and film
___ beverages

NOTE: This list does not include common art supplies (e.g., scissors, markers, glue, tape, pencils, hole punch), or cooking utensils (e.g., bowls, spoons, pans).

Bears

Happy Birthday Tara!

Patty   Katie

Stephanie

Teddy Bear Pattern

(page 62)

Getting Started

A great party depends on successful planning. Use this handy guide to help you get ready for the "beary" best party ever!

One Month Before the Party

____ Decide on day, time, and location.

____ Write a guest list. (Keep the number manageable.)

Two to Three Weeks Before the Party

____ Make a tentative schedule of party activities.

____ Buy (or make) and send out invitations. Include an RSVP. Have each child bring a favorite bear.

____ Make a list of decorations, food, and activity supplies.

____ Make or gather props for games.

____ Make or buy party decorations (e.g., banners, streamers, hats).

____ Buy colorful party table items (e.g., paper plates, cups, utensils, tablecloth, napkins).

____ Buy supplies needed for crafts.

____ Buy food items that do not need to be refrigerated.

____ Buy party bag treats and prizes.

____ Decide on an area for the games, crafts, food, and gifts.

Week of the Party

____ Finalize party schedule.

____ Call any guests who have not responded.

____ Buy last-minute foods and party supplies.

____ Borrow tables, chairs, and other needed items.

____ Prepare foods that can be made ahead of time (e.g., Honey Dip, raw vegetables).

____ Make a cake or order one.

____ Order balloons.

____ Prepare all games and activities.

____ Cut out craft patterns and prepare a bag or box of materials for each craft.

____ Select music (optional).

____ Check CD or cassette player, video recorder, and/or camera to be sure they're working.

Day of the Party

Four hours before

____ Pick up cake (if ordered).

____ Pick up balloons (if ordered).

____ Set the party table.

____ Set up prizes, games, crafts, and decorations.

One to two hours before

____ Organize music (optional).

____ Complete last-minute foods and drinks.

____ Make sure your child is dressed for the party and ready to greet guests.

____ Set out munchies.

____ Set out first craft.

As guests arrive

____ Greet guests and make them feel welcome.

____ Have paper and pen available to write down telephone or pager numbers where parents can be reached if needed.

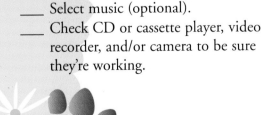

Chocolaty Bear Cake

Ingredients and Supplies

- 2 chocolate cake mixes
- milk chocolate frosting
- chocolate sprinkles or chocolate curls
- tubes of decorating icing
- sugar ice-cream cone
- beehives: vanilla frosting, chocolate jimmies, and yellow food coloring
- two 8" round cake pans
- cupcake tin
- cupcake liners
- mixing bowls
- knife
- cooling rack
- large platter

This "beary good" cake will get everyone in the party mood! Don't forget to use the extra cupcakes to make beehives. Your child's favorite ice cream would make a tasty addition to both.

Directions

1. Bake two round cakes and 10 to 12 cupcakes according to package directions.

2. Cool the cakes and cupcakes in the pans for 15 minutes. Take cakes out of the pans and cool completely on a rack.

3. Place the two round cakes on a platter to form the bear's head and body.

4. Place cupcakes on the top circle to form bear's ears. Add four cupcakes to the bear's body for paws and feet. (You may want to slice off the bottoms of the cupcakes to make them level with the bear's body.)

5. Slice the top off another cupcake and place it on the bear's face to form a snout.

6. Frost the bear cake with milk chocolate frosting. Add "fur" with chocolate sprinkles or chocolate curls. Place the ice-cream cone on the bear's head as a party hat. Add detail with decorating icing and other decorating materials.

Beehives

Use the remaining cupcakes to make beehives. Place vanilla frosting in a small bowl and mix in a few drops of yellow food coloring. Spread the yellow frosting on the cupcakes in swirled, beehive-like mounds. Sprinkle chocolate jimmies over the icing. Surround the bear cake with beehives. See page 65.

60

Party Foods

These tasty treats are sure to please a "beary hungry" crowd!

Honey Chicken Nuggets

Kids and bears alike love this finger- (and paw-) lickin' chicken entrée.

Ingredients and Supplies: 4 skinless chicken breasts (cut into nuggets), ½ cup melted butter, ½ cup honey, ¼ cup Dijon mustard (optional), ½ tsp salt, ½ tsp ground pepper, plain or seasoned bread crumbs, ranch dressing or barbecue sauce, cooking spray or butter, cookie sheet, shallow bowl

Directions

1. Preheat oven to 350°. Combine melted butter, honey, mustard, salt, and pepper in a shallow bowl.
2. Coat each chicken nugget with the honey mustard mixture and then roll in bread crumbs. Place each piece on a greased cookie sheet and bake about 20 minutes or until chicken is done. Serve with ranch dressing or barbecue sauce.

Variation: Buy frozen chicken nuggets. Prepare the nuggets as directed on the box and serve with honey.

Bear Claws

Ingredients and Supplies: 11-oz can of refrigerated breadstick dough, melted butter or margarine, basting brush, large cookie sheet, kitchen scissors or sharp knife

Directions

1. Preheat oven to 350°. Unroll dough and separate the eight pieces at the perforations.
2. Cut each piece of dough in half to make 16 smaller strips.
3. Place dough pieces on ungreased cookie sheet. Make two 1" cuts at the end of each piece and spread them apart to form "claws."
4. Bake claws for about 15 minutes or until golden brown, then brush each claw with melted butter.

Honey Dip

Ingredients and Supplies: ½ cup peanut butter, ¼ cup honey, ½ cup sour cream, fresh vegetables, apple slices, pretzels, small bowl, serving platter

Directions

1. Place the peanut butter, honey, and sour cream in a bowl and blend well.
2. Serve with fresh vegetables, apple slices, and pretzels.

Yummy Bear Treats

Have plenty of gummy bears and graham-cracker bears on hand. Place them in bowls on the party table, fill party bags, and use them as game prizes.

"Float" gummy bears in individual gelatin molds and place a few graham-cracker bears in ice cream.

Use prepared cookie dough or your favorite cookie recipe to make "beary good" cookies. To form each bear's body, drop a small mound of dough on a cookie sheet. Add smaller balls of dough for the head, ears, arms, and legs. Using your fingers, gently press the body flat, and make sure the bear parts are connected to the bear's body. Use extra chocolate chips or candy pieces for eyes, nose, and buttons.

Games and Activities

Introduce these games and activities, and have your camera ready to record the fun! Prizes, if any, should suit the ages of your guests as well as the theme. Consider stickers, small plastic bears, candies, and other bear-related items. Be sure each child receives several prizes.

Obstacle Course Ideas

- walk on two-by-fours
- crawl through large boxes
- hop in and out of hula hoops
- go around sprinklers
- crawl over plastic trash cans
- outdoor play equipment or other items you have or can easily borrow

Bear Hunt Obstacle Course Relay

Materials: two pairs of large-size heavy socks and mittens, fish cut from colorful construction paper with a lollipop taped to each (one per child), two bowls to hold fish, simple obstacle course items

Directions

1. Set up identical obstacle courses for two teams. Place a bowl of lollipop fish at the end of each course.
2. Divide players into two equal teams. On *Go!*, the first players in line put on bear paws (socks and mittens) and make their way (on hands and knees) through the course to the fish bowls. The players then each pick up a fish and carry it back through the obstacle course to the starting point.
3. When the first player on each team reaches the starting point, he or she takes off the paws and gives them to the next player.
4. The game continues until each player has run the course. The first team to finish wins.

Laughing Bears

Materials: none

Directions

1. Have guests sit in a circle. Tell them they must keep straight faces or they are "out" and must move to the inside of the circle. The birthday child begins the game by turning to the player on his or her left and doing something silly (e.g., making a funny face or striking a silly pose).
2. The player watching then turns to the next player and repeats the action. The game continues around the circle.
3. When each person has repeated the action, the person next to the birthday child becomes the leader and does something new.
4. Continue the game until only one straight-faced person is remaining. This player is the winner.

Teddy Bear Dress-Up

Invite partygoers to dress up the teddy bear friends they brought along to the party. Supply a large variety of items for them to use. Include doll clothes, baby clothes (purchased inexpensively at thrift stores or garage sales), party hats, costume jewelry, ribbons, fabric and felt scraps, tissue and crepe paper, and brown lunch bags or construction paper to make vests. When the bears are dressed, display them on or near the party table. While guests are engaged in other activities, fill out an award for each bear. Use the bear pattern (page 58) to make the awards extra special.

Decorations

Create an adorable and cozy look by sponge-painting a white paper tablecloth with colorful bears using a bear-shaped sponge. Use paper plates and napkins with a bear theme. Add toy bears of all shapes and sizes to the party table. Decorate the room with balloons printed with bear faces or draw them on with markers.

To welcome your guests, make an oversized bear by stuffing a pair of jeans and a plaid shirt with newspapers and rags. Add socks, boots, and gloves. Place a large teddy bear inside the shirt so that its head is sticking out. Place the stuffed bear on a chair outside the front door holding a welcome sign and balloons.

Bears Party Shopping List

Use this handy checklist to help you plan the items you'll need to buy or gather for your party. Check off items as you get them.

NOTE: This list does not include common art supplies (e.g., markers, glue, tape, pencils, scissors, hole punch) or cooking utensils.

Chocolaty Bear Cake *(page 60)*
- ___ 2 chocolate cake mixes
- ___ milk chocolate frosting
- ___ chocolate sprinkles or chocolate curls
- ___ decorating icing
- ___ sugar ice-cream cone

Beehive Cupcakes *(page 60)*
- ___ vanilla frosting
- ___ yellow food coloring
- ___ chocolate jimmies
- ___ cupcake liners

Honey Chicken Nuggets *(page 61)*
- ___ skinless chicken breasts
- ___ butter
- ___ honey
- ___ Dijon mustard (optional)
- ___ bread crumbs
- ___ ranch dressing or barbecue sauce
- ___ cooking spray

Bear Claws *(page 61)*
- ___ can of refrigerated breadstick dough
- ___ butter or margarine

Honey Dip *(page 61)*
- ___ peanut butter
- ___ honey
- ___ sour cream
- ___ vegetables, apple slices, pretzels

Yummy Bear Treats *(page 61)*
- ___ gummy bears
- ___ graham-cracker bears
- ___ gelatin
- ___ cookie dough
- ___ ice cream
- ___ chocolate chips and/or candy pieces

Stuffed Bear Party Bags *(page 62)*
- ___ 12" x 18" posterboard
- ___ brown wrapping paper
- ___ decorating materials
- ___ bear-themed party bag treats and toys
- ___ yarn
- ___ tissue paper

Happy Birthday Bear *(page 62)*
- ___ 2 sheets brown and 2 sheets white posterboard
- ___ construction paper
- ___ markers
- ___ decorating materials (e.g., tissue paper, foam paper, feathers, buttons, yarn, fabric scraps)

Bear Memory Books *(page 63)*
- ___ brown and white merchandise bags or lunch bags
- ___ brown and white construction paper
- ___ ribbon or yarn
- ___ bear-themed memory book supplies (e.g., stickers, die-cut shapes, colorful paper)
- ___ tan felt or foam paper (optional)

Teddy Bear T-shirts *(page 63)*
- ___ infant-size white T-shirts
- ___ fabric markers
- ___ newspapers

Face Painting *(page 63)*
- ___ face-painting kit

Bear Hunt Obstacle Course Relay *(page 64)*
- ___ two pairs heavy socks and mittens
- ___ construction paper
- ___ lollipops
- ___ obstacle course items

Teddy Bear Dress-Up *(page 64)*
- ___ doll and baby clothes
- ___ party hats
- ___ costume jewelry
- ___ ribbons, fabric, and felt scraps
- ___ brown lunch bags
- ___ paper (tissue, crepe, construction)

Decorations and Miscellaneous
- ___ invitations and thank-you notes
- ___ plates, cups, napkins, and utensils
- ___ tablecloths
- ___ balloons, streamers, and confetti
- ___ prizes and party bag fillers
- ___ camera and film
- ___ beverages

Outer Space

Spaceship Cake

Your party will blast off with this personalized cake! Kids will love having a spoonful of the "flame" on top of their serving.

Ingredients and Supplies

- cake mix of your choice
- prepared white frosting
- tubes of decorating icing (red, blue, brown)
- candy decorations
- edible glitter
- 1 cup whipped cream
- red and yellow food coloring
- 13" x 9" baking pan
- 12" x 8" sheet of waxed or baking paper
- large mixing bowl
- cooling rack
- sharp serrated knife
- serving platter
- Spaceship Cake Fin Pattern (page 68)
- toothpick

Directions

1. Mix the cake according to package directions. Bake in a 13" x 9" pan. To be sure the cake lifts out easily, place waxed or baking paper in the bottom of the baking pan before buttering or spraying.

2. Cool the cake for at least 10 minutes before turning out onto cooling rack. Peel off the waxed or baking paper. Allow the cake to cool completely.

3. Use the triangular spaceship fin pattern (page 68) to cut the two corners off the top of the cake. Arrange your spaceship and the corner fins on your serving platter.

4. Glue the fins to the body with frosting, then frost the entire cake.

5. Use a toothpick or knife point to lightly trace your decorating design. Decorate with tubes of icing, candies, and edible glitter.

6. Streak drops of red and yellow food coloring through the whipped cream and refrigerate.

7. Just before serving, spoon the colored whipped cream onto the platter in a flame shape at the base of the rocket.

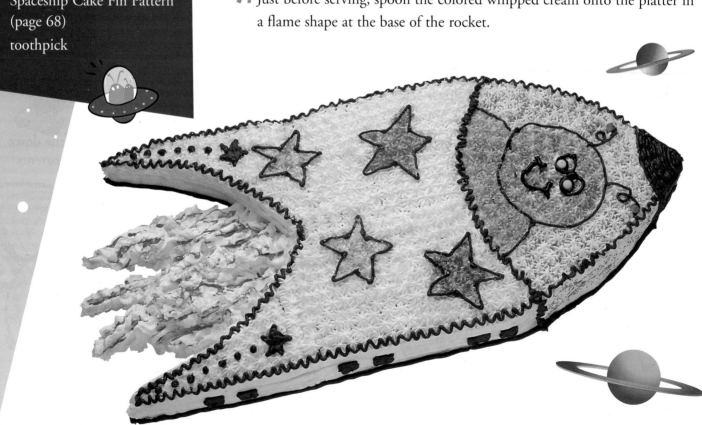

Party Foods

These far-out foods will delight your guests! Remember to round out the menu with your child's favorite chips, vegetables and dip, and fresh fruits.

Nebula Punch

Ingredients and Supplies: *2-liter bottle of lemon-lime soda, large can or carton of pineapple juice, lime sherbet, large punch bowl and serving ladle, plastic glasses, twisty straws, dry ice (optional)*

Note: Add dry ice to the punch just before serving for a cloudy effect. Look under "ice" in your local yellow pages for the nearest dealer. Special handling is necessary with dry ice. Read all cautions carefully.

Directions

1. Scoop sherbet into balls or cut into cubes; keep frozen. Refrigerate soda and juice. Keep dry ice well wrapped in freezer until needed.

2. At the time of the party, place sherbet pieces into punch bowl. Add soda and juice.

3. Using a protective mitt, place a chunk of dry ice in the punch and watch the clouds overflow the bowl. To get more clouds, break off the ice crust that forms.

4. Serve the punch with twisty straws. Make sure that no dry ice is poured into the cups.

Moon Pizzas

Assembled ahead of time, these take only eight to ten minutes to cook.

Ingredients and Supplies: *prepared pizza crusts, (large or individual sizes), prepared pesto sauce, shredded mozzarella cheese, drained black olive slices, pepperoni slices, baking sheet*

Variation: Use halved English muffins for pizza crusts.

Directions

1. Spread a thin layer of pesto sauce on pizza crusts.

2. Sprinkle most of the cheese over sauce.

3. Add olive and pepperoni slices.

4. Sprinkle remaining cheese on top.

5. Place on ungreased baking sheets and bake as directed on pizza crust packaging.

Blast-off Gelatin

Ingredients and Supplies: *blueberry-flavored gelatin (a 6-oz box makes 8 ½-cup servings), fresh fruit or canned fruit cocktail, whipped cream, 7-oz clear plastic cups, toy spaceships*

Directions

1. Prepare gelatin as directed on packaging, pour into plastic cups, and refrigerate.

2. When the gelatin is slightly thickened (about 45 minutes), stir fruit into each cup.

3. Refrigerate until firm.

4. Just before serving, add a blast of whipped cream. Top with a plastic spaceship.

Starry Trail Mix

Kids will have fun making trail mix to munch on during the party. Place small bowls of candy pieces, honey-roasted almonds, dried cranberries, and other tasty treats on a table. Invite guests to scoop a little of each treat into a resealable plastic bag. Write names on bags with a permanent marker.

Games and

Fun and games keep everyone moving—and happy! Prizes, if any, should suit the ages of your guests as well as the theme. Consider glow sticks, light-up yo-yos, freeze-dried fruits, stickers, and small space or alien toys. Be sure each child receives several prizes.

Black Hole Toss

Materials: Flying Saucers (page 74) or Frisbee-type throwing disks, large piece of foam board or heavy cardboard painted black (at least 28" x 40"), craft knife, white paint or white chalk and fixative spray, paintbrush

Directions

1. Cut out a circle (about 16" in diameter) from the middle of the black board. Decorate around the hole with white paint or chalk in a galactic design. If you use chalk, fix the color with spray to prevent smudging.

2. Fix the black board in a sturdy position, allowing space behind the board where saucers can be retrieved. Mark a line five to twelve feet away, depending on the ages of your guests.

3. Have guests take turns throwing their saucers through the black hole.

Catch the Comet

Materials: 2" to 3" balls of soft foam or Styrofoam, rubber bands (3 per child), 3' lengths of metallic-colored curling ribbon (3 to 5 per child), safety pins

Directions

1. Wrap three rubber bands around each comet ball.

2. Secure several ribbons under the rubber bands. (Do not tie the ribbons to the rubber bands.)

3. Attach a comet to the back of each child's waist by putting a safety pin through one of the rubber bands.

4. On *Go!*, have children run around trying to grab as many ribbons as they can. The game ends when all ribbons have been collected.

5. The winner is the person with the most ribbons.

New Twists on Old Favorites

Play a game of musical space chairs. Set the chairs up to form a spaceship and play *Star Wars*-type music.

Play this version of Pin the Tail on the Donkey: Draw a large version of the Spaceship Cake and attach it to the wall. Create flames from construction paper or streamers, and have children try to pin their flames on the spaceship.

Activities

Moon Rock Hunt

Materials: assortment of small rocks, silver spray paint

Directions

1. Spray the rocks with silver paint and allow them to dry completely.
2. Before guests arrive, hide the rocks throughout the party area.
3. Have children search for the rocks. Have a prize on hand for the child who finds the most rocks, or allow all the children to take their far-out rocks home with them.

Splashdown

Materials: five 3" rubber balls or small plastic rockets, bucket half-filled with water, blue plastic tablecloth, masking tape

Directions

1. Spread out the tablecloth in an area you won't mind getting a little wet. Place the bucket of water in the middle of it.
2. With the masking tape, mark a throwing line.
3. Invite children to take turns throwing five balls or rockets, trying to splash land in the "ocean."
4. Kids can collect a prize for successful landings.

Space Goop

Kids will love this mysterious substance!

Materials: 1-lb box of cornstarch, 1½ cups cold water, 1 tbsp green or blue food coloring, plastic dishpan or large bowl, waxed paper, small resealable plastic bags

Directions

1. Mix the cornstarch, water, and food coloring in a bowl with your hands until it is smooth. (Children love to help with this.)
2. Scoop a glob of goop onto waxed paper for each child. Let them touch, pound, and squeeze it. (Add a little more water if the goop gets too dry.)
3. Give each child a plastic bag so they can take some goop home. It will keep for several days if water is added as it dries.

Build Your Own Spaceship

Kids will have a blast building their own spaceships using various cardboard containers (e.g., cereal boxes, shoe boxes, paper tissue tubes), Styrofoam packing materials, and other lightweight containers. Use masking tape to fasten the pieces together. Spaceships can be lightly spray-painted white or gray. Black marker and decorative materials can be used to add details.

Outer Space Crafts

Children are proudest of the things they make themselves. They can start by making their own take-home Space Bags. If you have room, prepare a separate table with a plastic tablecloth for your craft projects and supplies.

Space Bags

Materials: colorful paper party bags, glitter-glue pens, construction paper scraps, blue pipe cleaners, space patterns (page 68), hole punch, marker, scissors

Directions

1. Open the bag and fold the top down twice to make a 1" rim.
2. Punch two holes on one side of the rim, about 1½" from the side edges. Repeat on the other side.
3. Decorate bags with glitter glue and various shapes cut from construction paper.
4. To make the bag's handles, thread a pipe cleaner through the holes on one side of the bag and twist the ends together to secure. Repeat on the other side.
5. Write children's names on bags with a marker.

Flying Saucers

Materials: heavy-weight paper plates (2 per child), stickers, paper scraps, stamps, space patterns (page 68), markers and crayons, stapler

Directions

1. Invite each child to decorate the backs of two paper plates.
2. Staple the two plates together at the rims.
3. Write children's names on the saucers with a marker.

Space Creatures

Materials: 8-oz foam cups, 2" Styrofoam balls cut in half, pipe cleaners, decorating materials (e.g., wiggly eyes, space stickers, aluminum foil scraps, silver beads), silver glitter glue

Directions

1. Turn the cup upside down. Glue a halved Styrofoam ball to the cup to make the creature's head.
2. Poke a long pipe cleaner through the cup to make the arms. Attach two smaller pieces to the head to form antennae.
3. Add features using decorating materials. (See samples on pages 67 and 69.)

Alien Masks

Masks may be funny, silly, or scary!

Materials: paper plates, elastic string, modeling clay, decorating materials (e.g., markers, crayons, glitter, stickers, paper scraps, pipe cleaners, ribbon pieces) hole punch, glue, scissors, stapler

Directions

1. Before the party, prepare a mask for each child. Cut eye holes in paper plates and punch holes near the sides to secure the elastic string.
2. Place all decorating materials on the craft table. Allow time for guests to decorate their masks as they please. Children can smear a small amount of clay on the masks to make "creepy" features.

Decorations

Create an out-of-this-world look by combining different materials. Use a dark blue tablecloth and aluminum foil for place mats. Sprinkle metallic confetti stars around. Use star garlands to decorate the chairs. Use paper plates with space themes, or different shapes of black or silver paper plates. Hang planets, stars, or spaceships from the light above the table.

To welcome your guests, hang silver and black balloons and streamers on the mailbox and the front door.

Outer Space Party Shopping List

Use this handy checklist to help you plan the items you'll need to buy or gather for your party. Check off items as you get them.

NOTE: This list does not include common art supplies (markers, crayons, pencils, glue, tape, scissors, hole punch, staplers) or cooking utensils (e.g., bowls, pans, knives, mixers, spoons).

Spaceship Cake *(page 70)*
___ cake mix
___ white frosting
___ tubes of decorating icing (red, blue, brown)
___ candy decorations
___ edible glitter
___ whipped cream
___ food coloring (red, yellow)
___ waxed or baking paper

Nebula Punch *(page 71)*
___ lemon-lime soda
___ pineapple juice
___ lime sherbet
___ twisty straws
___ dry ice (optional)

Moon Pizzas *(page 71)*
___ prepared pizza crusts
___ pesto sauce
___ shredded mozzarella cheese
___ black olives
___ pepperoni

Blast-off Gelatin *(page 71)*
___ clear plastic cups
___ blueberry-flavored gelatin
___ fresh fruit or canned fruit cocktail
___ whipped cream
___ toy spaceships for decoration

Starry Trail Mix *(page 71)*
___ candy pieces
___ honey-roasted almonds
___ dried cranberries
___ other treats of your choice

Black Hole Toss *(page 72)*
___ black foam board or heavy cardboard
___ craft knife
___ white paint or chalk and fixative spray
___ Flying Saucers (page 74) or Frisbee-type throwing disks

Catch the Comet *(page 72)*
___ 2" to 3" balls of soft foam or Styrofoam
___ rubber bands
___ metallic-colored curling ribbon
___ safety pins

Moon Rock Hunt *(page 73)*
___ silver spray paint
___ small rocks

Splashdown *(page 73)*
___ 3" rubber balls or small plastic rockets
___ blue plastic tablecloth
___ bucket

Space Goop *(page 73)*
___ cornstarch
___ food coloring
___ waxed paper
___ small resealable plastic bags

Space Bags *(page 74)*
___ paper party bags
___ glitter-glue pens
___ construction paper scraps
___ blue pipe cleaners

Flying Saucers *(page 74)*
___ heavy-weight paper plates
___ paper scraps
___ stickers and/or stamps

Space Creatures *(page 74)*
___ 8-oz foam cups
___ 2" Styrofoam balls
___ pipe cleaners
___ decorating materials (e.g., wiggly eyes, space stickers, aluminum foil scraps, silver beads)
___ silver glitter glue

Alien Masks *(page 74)*
___ paper plates
___ elastic string
___ modeling clay
___ decorating materials

Decorations and Miscellaneous
___ invitations and thank-you notes
___ tablecloths
___ plates, cups, utensils, and napkins
___ silver balloons, metallic streamers, and confetti
___ prizes or guest gifts
___ camera and film
___ music

Bugs

Critter Cake

Wow your guests with a cake that features colorful backyard critters!

Directions

1. Prepare the batter according to package directions. Bake in two 8" round pans and cool completely.

2. Add green food coloring to the vanilla frosting and frost the top of one cake.

3. Place the cake that is not frosted on top of the frosted cake to form a two-layer cake.

4. Using a sharp knife, score a 1½" border around the top layer of the cake. Scoop out the top portion of the cake to a depth of approximately ½".

5. Frost the sides of the cake and the top border with green frosting.

6. Prepare chocolate pudding according to package directions. Fill the depression with the pudding.

7. Arrange the gummy worms, candy sprinkles, and plastic bugs in and around the pudding to make a backyard garden scene.

Ingredients and Supplies

- chocolate cake mix
- prepared vanilla frosting
- green food coloring
- 4-oz package of chocolate pudding or pie filling
- gummy worms
- candy sprinkles
- plastic bugs
- two 8" round cake pans
- serving platter
- sharp knife
- spoon

Optional:
Use a cake decorating kit for added texture.

80

Party Foods

Burrowing Worms

Ingredients and Supplies: *hot dogs, hot dog buns, condiments (e.g., catsup, relish, mustard), knife, paper towels, saucepan*

Directions

1. Fill a saucepan with about one quart of water. Bring to a boil.

2. Cut six or seven slits along one half of each hot dog. Make the cuts about ¼" apart and ½" deep. Turn each hot dog over and make six or seven cuts on the opposite side.

3. Cook the hot dogs in boiling water about five minutes or until they become curvy. Remove from the water, and drain on paper towels.

4. Place the hot dogs on open buns. Serve with catsup, relish, and mustard.

Veggie Centipedes

Ingredients and Supplies: *cucumber, carrot, zucchini, cherry tomatoes (optional), 1 tbsp of cream cheese, raisins, dip, knife, large platter*

Directions

1. Slice cucumber and zucchini into circles. Overlap them on a platter to make several centipedes.

2. For the antennae and legs, cut thin slivers out of a carrot. Place cream cheese on one end of each sliver. Slide slivers behind several circles and press in place.

3. Use cream cheese to glue on raisins for eyes.

4. Serve with your favorite dip.

Peachy Critters

Ingredients and Supplies: *15-oz can of peach halves (makes about two bugs), 15-oz can of peach slices, thin licorice, white frosting, raisins, lettuce or cottage cheese (optional), lunch plates, toothpick*

Directions

1. If desired, line the plates with lettuce or cottage cheese.

2. Arrange three peach halves across each plate for the bug's body. Add six peach slices for legs—three on each side of the body.

3. For eyes, dip two raisins in the frosting, and glue them on the head. With a toothpick, make two holes in the head and insert two 2" licorice pieces for antennae.

Make-It-Yourself Bugs

Have party guests create their own critters. Here are two easy ideas to get them started. Toothpicks can be used to make holes for legs, arms, and so on.

Ingredients and Supplies: *large marshmallows, large gumdrops, miniature candies or candy sprinkles, thin licorice, white frosting, decorating icing, toothpicks*

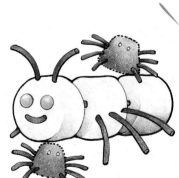

Gumdrop Spiders

Cut eight 1½" pieces of licorice for legs. Poke holes in the gumdrop body and insert licorice strips or glue on licorice with icing. Use drops of icing for eyes.

Marshmallow Ants

Cut two 1" pieces of licorice. Attach two marshmallows together by inserting one licorice piece between them. Attach a third marshmallow by inserting a second licorice piece. Insert six 3" pieces of licorice to the middle marshmallow for legs. Insert two 1" pieces of licorice to the marshmallow head for antennae. Add drops of icing, miniature candies, or candy sprinkles for eyes.

Games and

Treat children to these games and activities! Prizes, if any, should suit the ages of your guests as well as the theme of the party. Each child should receive several prizes. Consider stickers, pencils, small plastic bugs, gummy worms, small magnifying glasses, and other novelty items.

Bug Catchers

Bug catchers make perfect party favors for a bug party! Purchase plastic jars with lids—the kind used for storing food or knickknacks. Poke air holes in the lids and fill the jars with a variety of party favors. Have guests store their prizes in the jars. Allow time for children to decorate their containers with stickers.

Ladybugs and Aphids Relay

Materials: 2 large bowls of unshelled peanuts, 2 tablespoons, 2 large jars

Directions

1. Divide the group into two teams. Set a jar in front of each team. Set bowls of peanuts several yards away, one for each team.

2. Tell children that they are ladybugs looking for aphids (peanuts) to eat. Give the first child on each team a tablespoon. At your signal, the children with the spoons run to their bowls, scoop up some peanuts in the spoons, and walk back to their teams. Children empty the peanuts into their jars and then give the spoons to the next players. Spilled peanuts cannot be retrieved.

3. The game continues until everyone has had a chance to fetch peanuts.

4. Count the aphids in each jar. The team with the most aphids wins.

Bugs in a Jar

In this classic skills game, children see how many "bugs" they can drop into a jar.

Materials: plastic bugs, wide-mouthed jar, chair with a back

Directions

1. Place a jar on the floor directly below the back of a chair.

2. One at a time, children kneel on the chair so they can see the jar.

3. Give a child five plastic bugs. Have him or her try to drop them, one at a time, into the jar. Invite the child to count how many bugs fell into the jar. Make sure each guest gets a turn.

Activities

Grasshopper Leap Contest

Materials: sidewalk chalk, masking tape or jump rope (to mark starting and ending lines), tape measure, paper, pen or pencil

Directions

1. Divide the group into two or more equal teams.

2. Have each team stand behind a designated line.

3. The first player on the first team stands behind the line and then leaps as far as he or she can. Mark the spot where the child landed. The second player jumps from the spot where the first player landed; mark that spot for the third player. The activity continues until every player on the team has jumped.

4. Measure the distance from the starting line to the spot where the last child on the team landed. Write the distance on a sheet of paper.

5. Repeat steps 3 and 4 with each team. The team that leaps the farthest wins.

Hunt for Nectar

Materials: wrapped candy (10 per player), bags or Bug Catchers (1 per player)

Directions

1. Hide candy around the play area before the party starts.

2. When ready to play the game, tell children that they are bees hunting for nectar (candy).

3. Explain that they can search for ten pieces of candy and place them in their bags. Once a child has found ten candies, he or she can help other children find their candies.

Run, Ants, Run!

Here's a game that combines the fun of Follow-the-Leader and Tag.

Tell children that they are ants walking in a line. Have them follow a leader (an adult or another child) around the yard. (If you like, set up chairs, cones, and other obstacles for children to go around.) As children walk, the leader performs other actions for the "ants" to copy, such as hop on one foot or raise both arms up high. When the leader suddenly calls out *Run!*, children run to an area designated as "home." The leader tries to tag one or more children. Tagged children are out. The last person tagged becomes the next leader.

Crawly Crafts

Your guests will have loads of fun with these party crafts, and will also have some great keepsakes to take home. If you have room, prepare a separate table with a plastic tablecloth for your craft projects and supplies.

Antennae Headbands

Materials: plastic headbands, black pipe cleaners, black 1" pompoms, glue, thick felt marker, glitter (optional)

Directions

1. Twist pipe cleaners around the headband. Curl each one by twisting it around a thick marker and then sliding out the marker.

2. Dab some glue onto a pompom and insert one pipe cleaner into it. Squeeze the pompom to secure the pipe cleaner in place. Repeat with the other pompom and pipe cleaner.

Butterfly Memo Holders

You may want to complete steps 1 and 2 the day before the party.

Materials: Butterfly Pattern (page 78), craft foam, clothespins, 3" pieces of black pipe cleaner, sequins, craft eyes, craft glue, magnetic tape, scissors

Directions

1. Bend a pipe cleaner into a V-shape. Curl the ends to form the antennae. Glue it to the top of the clothespin and allow to dry.

2. Use the pattern to cut a butterfly shape, or create your own bug from craft foam.

3. Glue eyes onto the butterfly's head. Glue sequins and beads onto the body.

4. Glue the butterfly onto the clothespin. Glue a strip of magnetic tape to the back of the clothespin.

Walnut Roly-Poly Bugs

Materials: walnut shells (halved), cardboard, marbles, hole punch, craft eyes, scissors, pipe cleaners, pencil, felt markers, glue

Directions

1. Place a walnut shell on the cardboard. Trace the outline and cut out the cardboard.

2. Using the hole punch, punch several times into the middle of the cardboard to make an opening big enough for the marble to show through, but small enough so it won't fall out.

3. Place a marble inside the shell. Glue the cardboard onto the bottom of the shell.

4. Glue on pipe cleaner pieces and craft eyes. Decorate with markers and roll the bug on a flat surface.

Bead Caterpillars

Materials: pipe cleaners, tri-beads, round beads, scissors

Directions

1. Cut the pipe cleaner in half. Thread both pieces through a tri-bead. Bend up the ends of the pipe cleaner to secure the bead in place.

2. Thread pipe cleaners through beads, leaving about 1½" free.

3. Thread the second tri-bead through. Bend up the ends of the pipe cleaners to secure the beads. Curl the ends of the pipe cleaners to form antennae.

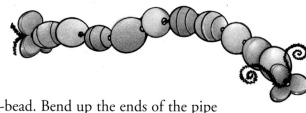

Decorations

Create a colorful party scene with an assortment of bugs! Hang streamers from the ceiling or from the top of a windowsill, and tape on bugs, butterflies, and other creatures made from construction paper. Decorate balloons with bug stickers, and hang them with ribbon near the party table. Use paper plates, cups, and napkins with a bug theme. Make Bead Caterpillars and Roly-Poly Bugs (see directions on page 84), and scatter them around the party table.

To welcome your guests, hang balloons and streamers on the mailbox.

Bugs Party Shopping List

Use this handy checklist to help you plan the items you'll need to buy or gather for your party. Check off items as you get them.

Critter Cake (*page 80*)
____ chocolate cake mix
____ vanilla frosting
____ green food coloring
____ 4-oz package of chocolate pudding or pie filling
____ gummy worms, gumdrops, other bug-like candies, and plastic bugs
____ candy sprinkles

Burrowing Worms (*page 81*)
____ hot dogs
____ hot dog buns
____ condiments (e.g., catsup, mustard, relish)

Veggie Centipedes (*page 81*)
____ cucumber
____ carrot
____ zucchini
____ cream cheese
____ raisins
____ dip

Peachy Critters (*page 81*)
____ 15-oz can of peach halves
____ 15-oz can of sliced peaches
____ thin licorice
____ white frosting
____ raisins
____ lettuce or cottage cheese (optional)

Make-It-Yourself Bugs (*page 81*)
____ large marshmallows
____ large gumdrops
____ miniature candies or candy sprinkles
____ thin licorice
____ white frosting
____ decorating icing

Bug Catchers (*page 82*)
____ plastic jars with lids
____ party favors (e.g., stickers, plastic bugs, gummy worms, small magnifying glasses)

Ladybugs and Aphids Relay (*page 82*)
____ unshelled peanuts
____ 2 large jars

Bugs in a Jar (*page 82*)
____ plastic bugs
____ wide-mouthed jar

Grasshopper Leap Contest (*page 83*)
____ sidewalk chalk, masking tape, or jump rope

Hunt for Nectar (*page 83*)
____ wrapped candy
____ bags or Bug Catchers

Antennae Headbands (*page 84*)
____ headbands
____ black pipe cleaners
____ 1" black pompoms

Butterfly Memo Holders (*page 84*)
____ craft foam
____ clothespins
____ black pipe cleaners
____ sequins
____ craft eyes
____ magnetic tape

Walnut Roly-Poly Bugs (*page 84*)
____ walnut shells
____ cardboard
____ marbles
____ pipe cleaners
____ craft eyes

Bead Caterpillars (*page 84*)
____ pipe cleaners
____ tri-beads
____ round beads

Decorations and Miscellaneous
____ invitations
____ thank-you notes
____ plates, cups, napkins, tablecloths, utensils
____ balloons, streamers and confetti
____ camera and film
____ music
____ beverages

NOTE: This list does not include common art supplies (e.g. markers, glue, tape, pencils, scissors, hole punch) or cooking utensils.

Construction

KIDS

KIDS

AT

PLAY

DAVEY Construction

FUN

AT

PLAY

Model Home Pattern

(page 93)

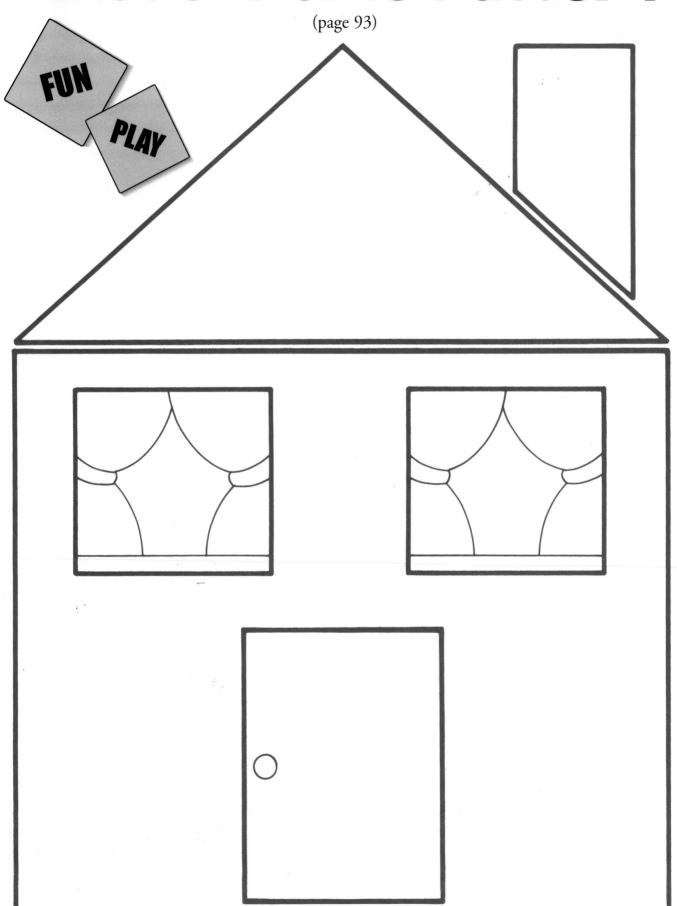

Getting Started

A great party depends on successful planning. Use this handy guide to help you get ready for the best Construction Party ever!

One Month Before the Party

___ Decide on the day, time, and location.
___ Write a guest list. (Keep the number manageable.)
___ Start collecting small boxes for the Build and Recycle project.

Two to Three Weeks Before the Party

___ Make a tentative schedule of party activities.
___ Buy (or make) and send out invitations. Include an RSVP and a request for empty small boxes for the Build and Recycle project.
___ Make a list of decorations, food, and activity supplies.
___ Collect or buy materials needed for games and projects.
___ Make or buy party decorations (e.g., banners, streamers, hats).
___ Buy nonperishable food items.
___ Buy colorful party table items (e.g., napkins, plates, cups, utensils, tablecloth).
___ Buy party favors and prizes.
___ Make game props and sample projects.
___ Decide which areas in your home will be used for projects, games, food, and gifts.
___ Select party music (optional).

Week of the Party

___ Finalize party schedule.
___ Call any guests who have not responded.
___ Buy last-minute foods and party supplies.
___ Borrow tables, chairs, sawhorses, and other needed items.

___ Prepare foods that can be made ahead of time.
___ Make a cake or order one.
___ Order balloons.
___ Cut out project patterns and prepare a bag of materials for each project.
___ Check CD or cassette player, video recorder, and/or camera to be sure they're working.

Day of the Party

Four hours before

___ Set the party table.
___ Set up decorations, games, and projects.
___ Pick up cake (if ordered).
___ Pick up balloons (if ordered).

One to two hours before

___ Review party schedule.
___ Organize music (optional).
___ Set out materials for the first project.
___ Complete last-minute foods and drinks.
___ Make sure your child is dressed for the party and ready to greet guests.

As guests arrive

___ Greet guests and make them feel welcome.
___ Have paper and pen available to write down telephone and pager numbers where parents can be reached if needed.

CAUTION Party Zone

Construction Zone Cake

Ingredients and Supplies

- cake mix of your choice
- prepared chocolate frosting
- yellow decorating icing
- green food coloring
- 6 Oreo cookies
- shredded coconut
- jelly beans or other small candies
- cookies-and-cream ice cream
- 13" x 9" baking pan
- small plastic dump truck and bulldozer
- birthday candles
- large mixing bowl and spoons
- measuring spoons
- large serving platter
- resealable plastic bags
- rolling pin
- knife
- paper towel
- craft stick, index card and tape (for sign)

You'll have a lot of fun constructing this cake—almost as much fun as your guests will have eating it! A scoop of cookies-and-cream ice cream makes a great addition.

Directions

1. Mix, bake, and cool the cake according to package directions.

2. To make "dirt," finely crumble the Oreo cookies by placing them in a resealable plastic bag and rolling over the bag with a rolling pin.

3. To make "grass," mix 1 teaspoon of water and a few drops of green food coloring in a plastic bag. Add coconut and shake well. Add more food coloring or water as needed to achieve desired color. Spread the coconut on a paper towel to dry.

4. Frost the cake. Sprinkle coconut grass on the cake, leaving a chocolate road. Make a center divider with yellow decorating icing.

5. Arrange dump truck, bulldozer, cookie dirt, and jelly beans on cake as desired.

6. Place candles along the road to resemble streetlights.

7. Write a special message on an index card and tape it to a craft stick. Insert this "billboard" in the grassy area.

FUN

Happy Birthday JOSE

PLAY

Note: Wash toy trucks in very warm water using dish soap and a tablespoon of liquid bleach. Rinse well.

Party Foods

This simple build-it-yourself menu has plenty to satisfy all tastes—and it looks good, too.

Build-Your-Own Sandwiches

Ingredients and Supplies: cocktail bread, deli meats, cheeses, tomato, lettuce, condiments, small serving plates or buckets (1 for each sandwich ingredient), clean (new) paintbrushes for spreading condiments

Directions

1. Cut all sandwich ingredients into small squares.

2. Place each ingredient on a plate or in a bucket.

3. Allow each guest to construct two to three small sandwiches.

Lumber Pile Fries

Ingredients and Supplies: frozen fried potatoes, baking sheet, metal or wooden tray

Directions

1. Cook fried potatoes as directed on package. Stack potatoes in piles on a metal or wooden tray.

2. Keep warm in oven until ready to serve.

Gelatin Bricks

Make the Jigglers recipe on the back of several flavors of Jell-O gelatin. When firm, cut into rectangular shapes. Stack "bricks" on a serving plate to resemble a colorful brick wall.

Fruit Towers

Ingredients and Supplies: pineapple, melon, apples, bananas, grapes, sweetened condensed milk, orange juice concentrate (2 tbsp), small bowl, paper plates, knife

Directions

1. Cut pineapple, melon, bananas, and apples into large cubes. Cut grapes in half.

2. Mix sweetened condensed milk and orange juice concentrate in small bowl to make a "cement" dip. Give each child several pieces of fruit and some dip.

3. Allow time for children to build and eat their towers.

Construction Punch

Ingredients and Supplies: orange juice, red tropical punch, and lemon-lime soda (2 quarts each); ice cube molds; punch bowl or mixing bowl; serving cups

Directions

1. Pour the orange juice into ice cube molds. Freeze until firm.

2. Mix the red punch and the soda in a punch bowl. Add the orange juice cubes.

3. When serving the punch, include a frozen cube in each cup.

Games and

Introduce these games and activities, and have your camera ready to record the fun! Prizes, if any, should suit the ages of your guests as well as the theme. Consider stickers, small trucks, candies, and other construction-related items. Be sure each child receives several prizes.

Construction Site Obstacle Course

Use materials you have on hand and in your imagination to make an enjoyable and safe obstacle course for partygoers.

Suggested Materials: two-by-four board to walk across, paint cans to walk around, sawhorses and plywood to crawl under, ladder or hoops to lay on the ground and jump through, sturdy boxes to climb over, packing boxes to crawl through, stopwatch (optional)

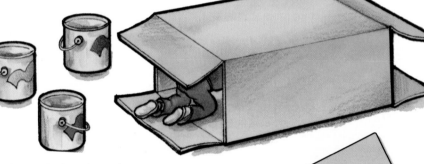

Directions

1. Demonstrate how to go through the obstacle course.

2. Have children take turns running the course.

3. To encourage competition, record individual or team times with a stopwatch and award prizes for the fastest time.

Construction Zones

Set up an outside construction zone for building and painting activities. Direct children there as they arrive and have them return there between activities. Children will love being construction workers, truck drivers, road pavers, and painters.

Building Materials: sandbox or wading pool, sand, building blocks, toy trucks, other sand toys

Directions

1. Place materials in a sandbox or wading pool filled with slightly damp sand.

2. Allow children to play at the construction site at various times during the party.

Painting Materials: large empty boxes such as appliance boxes and wardrobe boxes, washable paints, paintbrushes, several containers of water, baby wipes, cutting knife or scissors

Directions

1. Cut a door and window in each box to make a house.

2. Place paints, brushes, and water within children's reach.

3. Remind guests to place used brushes in water when they're finished painting, and have wipes available for quick cleanup.

Activities

Nuts and Bolts

Materials: dowel or stick, string, horseshoe magnet, large box or other container, nuts and bolts, pan or bucket, sawhorse, paper, pencil

Directions

1. Tie one end of the string to the stick or dowel and tie the other end to the magnet. Place a sawhorse, box with nuts and bolts, and pan in a game area as shown.

2. Have each child, in turn, go up to the sawhorse and swing the "crane" into the nuts and bolts box, picking up as many as the magnet will hold. The child then swings the nuts and bolts over to the pan.

3. A helper counts and records the number of items picked up and then returns them to the box.

4. Award a prize to the child who collects the most items.

Tract-Home Relay

Materials: model home pattern (page 88), posterboard, masking tape, marker, caution tape, scissors, two hard hats, game prizes

Directions

1. Choose an area for the race. Construct a model home pattern (as a guide for kids) and put up caution tape to designate a starting line.

2. Using the model home pattern as a guide, cut three of each piece from posterboard. Use one house as a sample and tape it to a fence or wall at the end of the playing area.

3. Divide the group into two even teams. Distribute one or two house pieces to each child. (Give the first two players on each team the triangular roof and the rectangular body of the house.)

4. Make sure each team has the necessary pieces to complete a house and that there is tape on the back of each piece.

5. On *Go!*, the first person on each team puts on a hard hat, runs to the wall, and tapes his or her piece next to the model home. The runner then returns to his or her team and hands the next person the hat. The first team to complete its house wins.

Note: For older kids, do not tape up a sample home, and add more house pieces such as steps, smoke from the chimney, and shutters for the windows.

Construction Projects

Your guests will have loads of fun with these party projects, and will also have some great keepsakes to take home. If you have room, prepare a separate table with a plastic tablecloth for your projects and supplies.

FUN

PLAY

Party Bags

Choose one of the ideas below to create memorable party bags for each guest. Write a child's name on each hat, brick, or belt. Place some party items (e.g., stickers, candies, rubber stamps, toy trucks) in the containers and have them available for children to store prizes they gather throughout the party.

Hats: Fill plastic hard hats with party items. Before kids leave the party, wrap the hats in transparent plastic wrapping paper and tie them off with ribbon.

Bricks: Make bricks by covering shoe boxes with self-adhesive brick-patterned shelf paper or painting them a brick-red color. Fill the boxes with party favors. Stack the bricks to form a wall.

Belts: Buy inexpensive toy tool belts and fill them with party items.

Gumdrop Structures

Materials: gumdrops and/or marshmallows (15 to 25 per child), toothpicks, 8" x 11" pieces of cardboard or heavy card stock (1 per child), glue, 2 bowls

Directions

1. Place gumdrops and toothpicks in bowls.
2. Demonstrate to younger guests how to poke toothpicks through gumdrops.
3. Allow time for children to create their structures.
4. Glue each structure to a piece of cardboard for display.

Build and Recycle

Materials: assorted cardboard containers (e.g., paper tubes, sample-size cereal boxes), various colors and textures of decorating paper (e.g., stiffened felt, foam paper, construction paper, tissue paper, aluminum foil), glue, scissors

Directions

1. Cut decorating paper into various shapes and sizes.
2. Allow time for partygoers to construct various structures or construction vehicles using the available materials.

Another Great Idea

Check your local craft or hobby store for inexpensive building kits. Birdhouses, decorative boxes, and other kits are fun to use as party projects or prizes.

FUN

PLAY

94

Decorations

A garage, an unfinished room, or your backyard are great places to have a Construction Party. Use sawhorses and plywood for tables. Decorate the party areas with yellow plastic "Caution" tape, yellow and black balloons, and road signs made from construction paper. Use cardboard covered with wood-grained adhesive paper for place mats. Choose yellow or black plates, cups, and utensils to enhance the party's theme. Game and project areas can be coned off with stacked packing boxes and/or orange cones.

To welcome your guests, hang balloons and streamers on the mailbox and front door, and post a sign directing them to the "Construction Zone."

Construction Party Shopping List

Use this handy checklist to help you plan the items you'll need to buy or gather for your party. Check off items as you get them.

NOTE: *This list does not include common art supplies (e.g., markers, crayons, tape, scissors) or utensils.*

Construction Zone Cake *(page 90)*
____ cake mix
____ chocolate frosting
____ yellow decorating icing
____ green food coloring
____ Oreo cookies
____ shredded coconut
____ jelly beans or other small candies
____ cookies-and-cream ice cream
____ small plastic dump truck and bulldozer
____ birthday candles
____ craft stick
____ index card

Build-Your-Own Sandwiches *(page 91)*
____ cocktail bread
____ deli meats and cheeses
____ tomato and lettuce
____ condiments
____ small buckets
____ clean, new paintbrushes

Lumber Pile Fries *(page 91)*
____ frozen fried potatoes

Gelatin Bricks *(page 91)*
____ flavored gelatin packages

Fruit Towers *(page 91)*
____ pineapple
____ melon
____ apples
____ bananas
____ grapes
____ sweetened condensed milk
____ orange juice concentrate
____ paper plates

Construction Punch *(page 91)*
____ orange juice
____ red tropical punch
____ lemon-lime soda
____ ice cube molds

Construction Site Obstacle Course Suggestions *(page 92)*
____ two-by-four board
____ paint cans
____ sawhorses
____ plywood
____ ladder or hoops
____ boxes
____ stopwatch (optional)

Construction Zones *(page 92)*
____ sandbox or wading pool
____ sand
____ building blocks
____ toy trucks
____ other sand toys
____ large boxes
____ paint and paintbrushes
____ baby wipes

Nuts and Bolts *(page 93)*
____ dowel or stick
____ string
____ horseshoe magnet
____ nuts and bolts
____ large box
____ pan or bucket

Tract-Home Relay *(page 93)*
____ posterboard
____ 2 hard hats

Party Bags *(page 94)*
Hats
____ plastic hard hats
____ transparent wrapping paper
____ ribbon
Bricks
____ shoe boxes
____ self-adhesive, brick-patterned shelf paper or red paint
Belts
____ toy tool belts

Gumdrop Structures *(page 94)*
____ toothpicks
____ gumdrops and/or marshmallows
____ cardboard or heavy card stock

Build and Recycle *(page 94)*
____ assorted cardboard containers
____ decorating paper

Decorations and Miscellaneous
____ invitations and thank-you notes
____ plates, cups, napkins, tablecloths, utensils
____ sawhorses
____ balloons, streamers, and confetti
____ prizes and party bag fillers
____ camera and film
____ beverages

Tea Party

Crepe-Paper Flower Patterns

(page 103)

Petal Pattern

Leaf Pattern

Teapot Pattern

(page 102)

Getting Started

A great party depends on successful planning. Use this handy guide to help you get ready for the best Tea Party ever!

One Month Before the Party
___ Decide on day, time, and location.
___ Write a guest list. (Keep the number manageable.)

Two to Three Weeks Before the Party
___ Make a tentative schedule of party activities.
___ Buy (or make) and send out invitations. Include an RSVP. Invite children to bring their favorite doll to the party.
___ Make a list of decorations, food, and activity supplies.
___ Make or buy party decorations (e.g., banners, streamers).
___ Buy items needed for games and crafts.
___ Buy colorful party table items (e.g., paper plates, cups, utensils, tablecloths, napkins, artificial ivy).
___ Buy food items that do not need to be refrigerated.
___ Buy party bag treats and prizes.
___ Make props and items for games.
___ Decide on an area for the games, crafts, food, and gifts.
___ Select party music (optional).

Week of the Party
___ Finalize party schedule.
___ Call any guests who have not responded.
___ Buy last-minute foods and party supplies.
___ Borrow tables, chairs, and other needed items.

___ Prepare foods that can be made ahead of time. (Pinwheel Sandwiches, Gelatin Flowers, and candy dishes can be prepared the day before.)
___ Make Heavenly Cupcakes or order a cake.
___ Order balloons.
___ Cut out craft patterns and prepare a bag or box of materials for each craft.
___ Prepare all games and activities.
___ Check CD or cassette player, video recorder, and/or camera to be sure they're working.

Day of the Party
Four hours before
___ Set the party table.
___ Set up decorations, games, and crafts.
___ Pick up cake (if ordered).
___ Pick up balloons (if ordered).

One to two hours before
___ Make sure your child is dressed for the party and ready to greet guests.
___ Complete last-minute foods and drinks.
___ Organize music (optional).
___ Set out snacks.

As guests arrive
___ Greet guests and make them feel welcome.
___ Have paper and pen available to write down telephone or pager numbers where parents can be reached if needed.

Heavenly Cupcakes

These dainty cupcakes are easy to make and beautiful to behold!

Directions

1. Prepare the batter according to the directions on the cake mix box.

2. Pour the batter into lined cupcake tins. Bake according to package directions. Cool thoroughly.

3. In the top of each cupcake, cut a circle about 2" in diameter and ½" deep.

4. To scoop out the circle, hold the knife at a slant and cut around the circle. The part that lies below the circle will be cut into the shape of a cone. Take off the top and set it aside.

5. Prepare the pudding according to package directions.

6. Fill the hole in each cupcake with pudding. Gently place the tops of the cupcakes onto the pudding.

7. Using the tea strainer as a sifter, lightly sift powdered sugar onto the tops of the cupcakes.

8. Using decorating icing, squeeze a flower shape onto each cupcake or top with candy sprinkles. Place dessert decorations in the pudding.

Ingredients and Supplies

(Makes 20–24 cupcakes)

- cake mix (yellow, white, chocolate, or butter)
- 4-oz package of instant pudding/pie filling
- tube of colored decorating icing and/or candy sprinkles
- powdered sugar
- dessert decorations
- cupcake liners
- cupcake tins
- tea strainer
- knife
- mixing bowl and spoon

Party Foods

Create an elegant tea party by serving delicious finger foods with iced tea, lemonade, or punch in a ceramic teapot. Be sure to let the birthday child pour the first cup.

Pinwheel Sandwiches

Ingredients and Supplies: white or wheat bread slices, peanut butter, honey or jam, cream cheese spread, sunflower seeds, cooked chicken, celery, mayonnaise, canned tuna, relish, knife, toothpicks, serving tray

Sandwich Fillings: peanut butter and honey or jam; cream cheese spread and sunflower seeds; minced cooked chicken, chopped celery, and mayonnaise; canned tuna, relish, and mayonnaise

Directions

1. Cut away the crust from each slice of bread.

2. Spread sandwich filling over each slice.

3. Roll up the bread tightly. Cut each slice into fourths and secure with a toothpick. Cover and keep chilled until serving time.

Gelatin Flowers

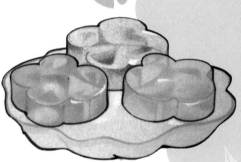

Ingredients and Supplies: two different 6-oz packages of flavored gelatin, 2 cups boiling water, two 8" square pans, flower-shaped cookie cutter, 2 mixing bowls, measuring cup, serving dish

Directions

1. In a bowl, pour 1 cup of boiling water over one flavored gelatin. Stir until the gelatin is completely dissolved. Repeat the procedure with the other gelatin in the other bowl.

2. Pour each gelatin mixture into a baking pan. Chill for at least three hours.

3. Place each pan in warm water for 15 seconds to loosen the gelatin. Use the cookie cutter to cut out flower shapes. Arrange the gelatin flowers on a serving dish.

Elegant Fruit Platter

Add a little elegance to a fruit platter by making lemon roses. Just cut around a lemon to form a thin spiral of peel. Make the spiral as long as possible. Starting at one end of the peel, begin curling to make the shape of a rose. Place three or four lemon roses on a platter filled with bite-sized pieces of fruit. Poke toothpicks in fruit pieces to make them easier (and more fun) to eat.

More Finger Foods

Spread butter or peanut butter on Ritz crackers. Place thinly sliced banana pieces on the crackers. Top some of the banana pieces with another cracker.

Serve candies, mints, nuts, and/or chocolates in decorative glass bowls, trays, or gold plastic serving dishes.

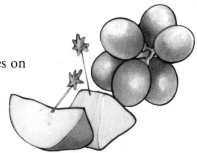

Tea Party

Delight your guests with these fun craft ideas! If you have room, prepare a separate table with a plastic tablecloth for your craft projects and supplies.

Pretty Party Bags

Present children with a variety of feminine treasures (e.g., costume jewelry, candy necklaces, play makeup, fingernail polish, stickers). Place the items in floral gift bags or small baskets.

Guest Book

As children arrive, have them sign their names, write a message to the birthday child, and/or draw a picture in this special guest book. For an extra-special effect, use a feathered pen or one that has gold or silver ink.

Materials: teapot pattern (page 98), 6" x 8" piece of stiffened felt or colored card stock (for teapot), two 8 ½" x 9 ½" pieces of stiffened felt or colored card stock (for book covers), 8 ½" x 9 ½" pieces of white paper (1 piece per guest), rickrack, ribbon, scraps of stiffened felt or colored card stock, glue, pencil, scissors, hole punch, fancy pen

Directions

1. Trace the teapot pattern onto the felt or card stock. Cut out the teapot.
2. Glue the teapot onto the front cover of the book.
3. Punch two holes at the top of the two covers. Punch holes in identical spots at the top of the pieces of white paper.
4. Assemble the book covers and white paper. Thread a ribbon through the holes and tie it into a bow.
5. Decorate the cover by gluing on scraps of felt or card stock and rickrack.

Colorful Jewelry

Materials: variety of beads, lacing or fishing wire, stick-on earrings, small stand-up mirrors or wall mirror

Directions

Invite guests to string beads for necklaces and bracelets to wear during the party. Provide stick-on earrings for children to wear. Place mirrors nearby so children can see how they look in their new jewelry.

Variation: Make edible jewelry using string licorice, ringed cereal, and ringed candies.

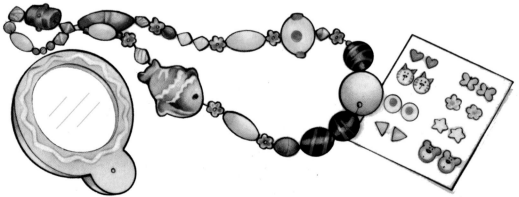

Crafts

Crepe-Paper Flowers

Make several crepe-paper flowers ahead of time, and place them in a vase as a colorful centerpiece for the party table. For younger children, make enough flowers before the party so that each child can take one home as a party favor. For older children, pre-cut patterns and have materials available for them to create their own flowers.

Materials (per flower): petal and leaf patterns (page 98), crepe paper cut into 5 or more 3" squares, 6" crepe-paper square of contrasting color, 2 or 3 pieces of green tissue paper cut into 3" squares (for leaves), 10" florist's wire or skewers, florist's tape or clear tape, scissors, glue

Directions

1. Fold the 6" crepe-paper square in half twice to make a narrow rectangle.

2. Wrap the crepe-paper rectangle around one end of the wire or skewer and tape in place to form the flower's center.

3. Use the petal pattern to cut out at least five petals from crepe paper. Using a dab of glue, attach the petals around the flower's center. (See samples on page 105.)

4. Wrap florist's tape completely around the wire to make the stem.

5. Use the leaf pattern to cut leaves from tissue paper. Fold each leaf in half to make a crease. Glue the leaves in place.

Classy Picture Frames

A tea party presents the perfect opportunity for picture taking! Take an instant photo of each child dressed up (see Dress-up Fun, page 104). If an instant camera is not available, send the photos later along with a thank-you note, or ask a helper to take the film to a one-hour photo processing center during the party.

Materials: acrylic picture frames, opaque paint markers, stickers, smocks or aprons to protect party clothes, camera, film

Directions

1. Decorate around the edges of the frames with the paint markers and stickers.

2. When the paint has completely dried, insert the photos for a special take-home treat!

Decorative Hair Accessories

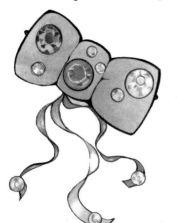

Materials: plain headbands and/or barrettes, decorative materials (e.g., sequins, jewels, glitter, ribbon roses, bows, buttons), tacky glue or glue gun

Directions

1. Allow each child time to choose a hair accessory and decorative materials.

2. Glue on various materials to make unique hair accessories.

Note: A glue gun works great for this project. If using a glue gun, have guests plan their designs before assisting them with the glue. Use caution when handling hot glue.

Games and Activities

Introduce these games and activities to partygoers and have your camera ready to record the fun!

Autograph Bingo

Here's a fun icebreaker that lets children get to know one another!

Materials: 8½" x 11" sheets of paper, pencils, thin black marker, ruler, party favor prizes

Directions for Bingo Cards

(Prepare these cards before the party.)

1. Draw a grid on an 8½" x 11" sheet of paper. Each grid should have three equal columns and three equal rows, as shown.

2. In the center space, write *My Name* and draw a line for the child to write her name.

3. In the remaining eight spaces, write phrases that describe the children attending the party. Leave enough room for a child to write her name below each phrase.

4. Photocopy a bingo card for each guest.

has flown on a plane	plays an instrument	has a pet
has a middle name	Hannah *my Name*	has visited another country
speaks two languages	made the bed today	has a sister

Playing the Game

1. Give each child a bingo card and a pencil. Have children write their names in the center space of their cards.

2. Have each child walk around the room and ask another guest if she can answer "yes" to any of the phrases. If she can, she writes her name in the appropriate space. For example, if the child can speak two languages, she writes her name in the space marked "speaks two languages."

3. Encourage children to get the autographs of as many guests as possible. Give a candy necklace or other treat as a reward for completing the cards.

Makeup Center

Materials: children's makeup, nail polish, lip gloss, stick-on fingernail decorations, mirrors, cotton swabs (for application)

Directions

Arrange makeup items on a table. Let two guests take turns putting on makeup. Stand by so that you can help the children put on blush, eye shadow, lip gloss, nail polish, and fingernail stickers.

Dress-up Fun

Materials: large boxes or baskets, an assortment of clothes and accessories (e.g., feather boas, hats, scarves, capes, shawls, belts, costume jewelry, barrettes, headbands, purses, shoes)

Directions

Sort similar items in large boxes or baskets, and invite children to go through the boxes to find things to wear. Have girls dress up and put on a fashion show!

Fancy Fashion Show

Mark out a runway on the floor with masking tape. Have children wear any jewelry they made along with the clothing and accessories you've provided. As children line up to walk down the runway, play background music. Comment on what each child is wearing as she walks down the runway.

Setting the Table

Cover the party table with a pretty tablecloth. If you like, spread a sheet of clear, stiff plastic (available at fabric stores) or a clear shower curtain liner over the tablecloth to protect it from spills. For dishes, use a child's tea set and inexpensive china cups, saucers, and plates found at garage sales and discount stores. Don't worry if the teacups don't match—a variety of patterns will add color and interest to the table setting!

Set out fancy dinner napkins and gold or silver napkin rings. If you don't want to use real silverware, buy fancy plastic cutlery at a party store or glue craft jewels onto plastic forks and spoons. Line plates with doilies and include a colorful vase of crepe-paper (page 103) or freshly cut flowers. Trim the table and chairs with artificial ivy vines for a garden look.

Buried Treasure Cake

Your pint-sized pirates will love uncovering the hidden treasures on this island!

Ingredients and Supplies

- cake mix of your choice
- prepared vanilla frosting
- green and blue food coloring
- edible glitter
- gummy candies
- small chocolate candies
- plastic pirates and a treasure chest
- gold-wrapped chocolate coins
- two 8" square (or round) cake pans
- melon baller
- green candles
- knife
- serving platter

Directions

1. Mix, bake, and cool the cake according to package directions.

2. Transfer one of the cakes to the serving platter. Carefully scoop out several areas of the cake using a melon baller. Fill the holes of the cake with small chocolate candies.

3. Add the blue food coloring to some of the vanilla frosting, and ice this layer to look like water.

4. Cut the second cake in a free-form pattern to resemble an island. Be sure this layer is smaller than the bottom layer but big enough to cover the candy-filled holes. Center the island on top of the holes.

5. Add the green food coloring to the remaining vanilla frosting, and ice the island.

6. Add plastic pirates, a treasure chest, chocolate coins, gummy candies, and edible glitter.

7. Add green candles for palm trees and write a birthday message with icing.

Note: The cakes will be easier to cut and frost if first placed in the freezer for 20 minutes.

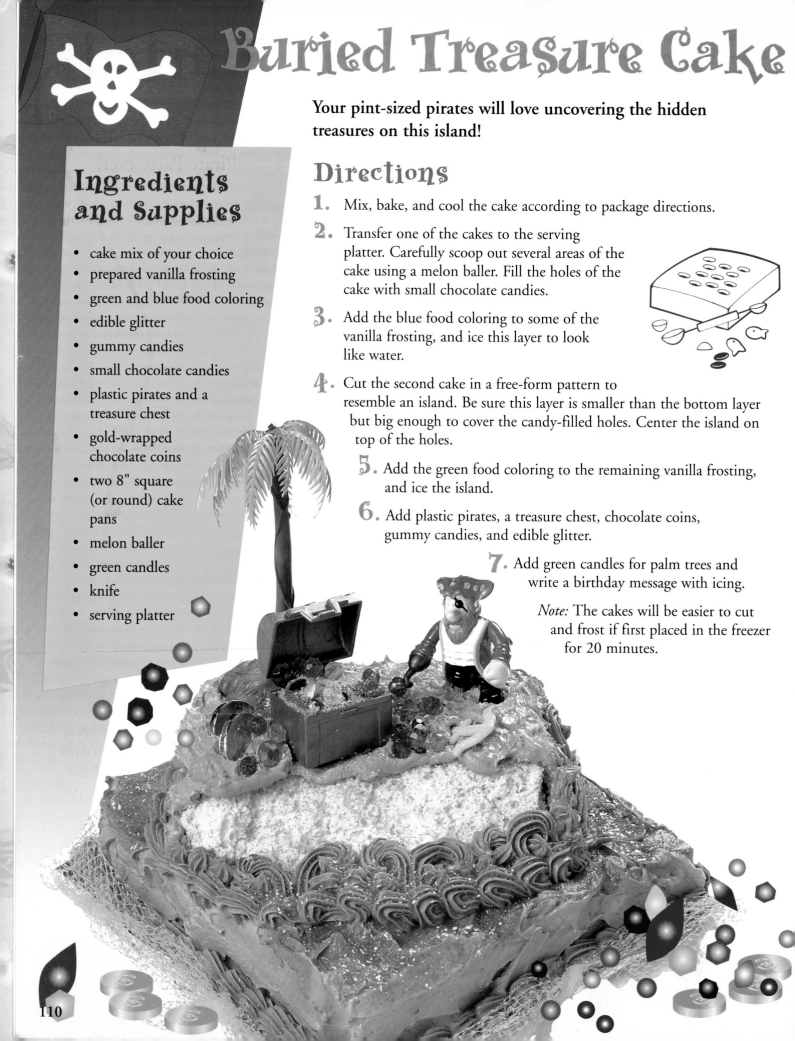

Party Foods

Ahoy, Matey! Keep your hungry band of sea dogs happy with these tempting treats!

Pirate Pinwheels

Ingredients and Supplies: large flour tortillas, softened cream cheese, assorted lunch meats and/or cheeses, knife, toothpicks, colored paper, scissors, glue

Directions

1. Spread a thin layer of cream cheese on tortillas.
2. Top with a layer of lunch meat and/or cheese.
3. Roll up and secure with toothpicks.
4. Refrigerate for at least one hour. Cut into 1" slices before serving.
5. Garnish with "masts" made by gluing paper triangles to toothpicks.

Variation: Use mayonnaise, mustard, or other condiments instead of cream cheese.

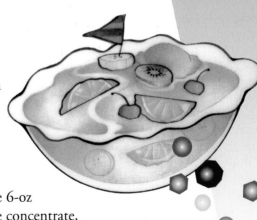

Peanut Butter Planks

Ingredients and Supplies: celery, peanut butter, raisins or chocolate chips, cutting board, knife

Directions

1. Wash celery and cut into 6" pieces.
2. Fill each piece with peanut butter.
3. Top with raisins or chocolate chips.

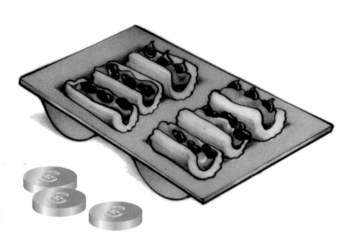

Buccaneer Banana Bread

Ingredients and Supplies: 3 ripe bananas, 1 egg, ½ cup melted butter, 1 cup sugar, 1½ cups flour, 1 tsp salt, 1 tsp baking soda, loaf pan, spoon, fork, 2 mixing bowls, cooking spray, toothpick

Directions

1. In a large bowl, mash bananas with a fork.
2. Beat the egg. Add the egg and the melted butter to the bananas and mix well.
3. In a small bowl, mix remaining ingredients and add to banana mixture.
4. Pour into a greased loaf pan and bake at 325° for 1¼ hours or until toothpick comes out clean.

Note: For an extra treat, add one cup chocolate chips, blueberries, or chopped nuts.

Pirate Punch

In a large punch bowl, mix a 32-oz can of pineapple juice, one 12-oz can of orange juice concentrate, one 6-oz can of lemonade concentrate, five cups of cold water, one quart of 7-Up, and one quart of rainbow sherbet. Chill until ready to serve. Add slices of orange, banana, or kiwi, or float cherries in the bowl for an added twist.

Games and

These games and activities will be sure to bring out the buccaneer in every child. Prizes, if any, should suit the age range of your guests as well as the theme of the party. Each child should receive several prizes. Consider stickers, pencils, eye patches, gold (chocolate) coins, compasses, candies, small plastic treasures, and other novelty items.

Walk the Plank

Materials: 5' plank of wood, fifteen 3" x 3" squares of paper, tape, pirate hat, 3 squares of cardboard, marker

Directions

1. Before the party, label a cardboard square *1*, another *2*, and the remaining square *3*. Place the pieces in a pirate hat.

2. Place the plank of wood on the floor. Draw footprints on the 15 paper squares. Tape the squares on the plank from end to end to make a path.

3. Invite the children to sit in a circle around the plank and the birthday child to stand at the beginning of the plank. One child from the circle pulls a number from the hat and asks the birthday child to walk that number of steps down the plank. Then the number drawn is put back in the hat and it is passed to the next child in the circle. The round continues until everyone in the circle has picked a number. If the birthday child is still on the plank, he or she has "survived" and wins a prize.

4. Have each child, in turn, be the plank walker.

Pin the Pirate

Materials: black construction paper, large piece of drawing paper, white chalk, markers, double-sided tape, blindfold

Directions

1. Before the party, draw a large pirate face on the drawing paper. Cut out eye patches (at least one per guest) from black paper. Hang the drawing at children's eye level.

2. At the party, pass out the eye patches and white chalk to partygoers.

3. Have each child choose a pirate name and sign an eye patch with it. Stick a piece of double-sided tape to the back of each patch.

4. Blindfold the birthday child. Spin him or her around three times, then point the child toward the drawing of the pirate face. Have the child stick the eye patch on the face. Continue until every child has had a turn.

5. The child with the eye patch closest to an eye is the winner.

Activities

Pass the Treasure

Materials: 5 to 10 boxes of various sizes, wrapping paper, assorted candies or small prizes, scissors, tape, music

Directions

1. Before the party, fill the smallest box with the candies or prizes. Wrap the box and place it in the next largest box. Continue until all the boxes are wrapped and placed inside one another.

2. At the party, invite the children to sit in a circle. Turn on some music and ask the children to pass the treasure. Stop the music from time to time. Whoever is holding the treasure when the music stops gets to open the package. Won't children be surprised to find another wrapped package!

3. Play continues until all the packages are unwrapped. When the treats are discovered, be sure all partygoers get some of the treasure.

Treasure Hunt

Materials: small prizes and candy, small bags or Treasure Chests (page 114)

Directions

1. Before the party, hide the prizes in a large room or backyard. Keep the children out of the area until the game begins.

2. Tell the children a story about buried treasure that has never been found. Then send them into the area and invite them to search for the treasure.

3. After all the treasures are found, children can put their trove in small bags or Treasure Chests.

Captain Kid Says

Play a pirate version of Simon Says. Dress the birthday child in a pirate's hat and clothes to play Captain Kid. When he or she makes the statement "Captain Kid says (put your hands on your head, etc.)," children are to follow the instructions. Any time Captain Kid doesn't start out with "Captain Kid says," all children who follow the instructions are out. Play continues until only one player is left standing. He or she becomes the new Captain Kid.

Tales of the Seven Seas

Busy buccaneers will welcome some quiet listening time with any of these pirate adventures:

Edward and the Pirates by David McPhail
Pirate Soup by Mercer Mayer
Peter Pan by James M. Barrie
The Pirate Queen by Emily McCully
One-Eyed Jake by Pat Hutchins

Pirate Crafts

Crafty pirates will enjoy making some great keepsakes to take along on their next adventure. If you have room, prepare a separate table with a plastic tablecloth for your craft projects and supplies.

Treasure Chests

Materials: small shoe boxes; self-adhesive paper, gold metallic wrapping paper, or aluminum foil; decorating materials (e.g., plastic jewels, stickers, gold cord, shiny ribbons, sequins); glue

Directions

1. Before the party, cover each box with self-adhesive paper, wrapping paper, or aluminum foil, and write a guest's name on each box.

2. At the party, pass out a covered box to each child. Invite children to decorate their treasure chests with decorating materials.

3. After the glue dries, children can fill their treasure boxes with the treats and prizes they accumulate throughout the party.

Variation: Glue, tape, or staple two 2" strips of ribbon to the box to make hinges.

Pirate Ships

Materials: Styrofoam bowls, craft sticks, glue, white paper, scissors, markers or crayons, basin of water (optional)

Directions

1. Give each child a bowl to serve as the ship's hull.

2. Have them cut out rectangles from the paper for sails and decorate the sails with markers or crayons.

3. Glue the sails onto the masts (craft sticks).

4. Have children place a small amount of glue at the bottom of each stick before carefully inserting it into the hull.

More Fun: Have a floating parade in a small plastic pool or a large basin.

Pirate Hats

Materials (for one pirate hat): 3 pieces of black stiffened felt or foam paper, pirate hat pattern (page 108), felt scraps in assorted colors, gold cord, feather, stapler, glue, scissors

Directions

1. Before the party, cut three pirate hat patterns for each guest from stiffened felt or foam paper. Staple the pieces together as shown on the pattern.

2. Invite children to decorate their hats with the felt scraps, gold cord, and a feather. Encourage them to design their own pirate logo to replace the traditional skull and crossbones.

Decorations

Choose plates, cups, utensils, and a tablecloth to enhance the party's pirate theme. Add color and excitement to your party table with balloons, streamers, and chocolate coins. Hang balloons in bunches near the table, from the backs of chairs, or from a light above the table. For a festive effect, place streamers on the table or drape them from a string hung above the table. Add pirate props such as plastic jewels, hats, and coins.

To welcome your guests, hang black and white balloons, streamers, and a skull and crossbones made from construction paper on the mailbox and front door.

Pirate Party Shopping List

Use this handy checklist to help you plan the items you'll need to buy or gather for your party. Check off items as you get them.

NOTE: This list does not include common art supplies (e.g., markers, glue, tape, pencils, scissors, hole punch), cooking utensils or toothpicks.

Buried Treasure Cake *(page 110)*
- ___ cake mix
- ___ prepared vanilla frosting
- ___ green and blue food coloring
- ___ edible glitter
- ___ gummy candies
- ___ small chocolate candies
- ___ plastic pirates and a treasure chest
- ___ gold-wrapped chocolate coins
- ___ green candles

Pirate Pinwheels *(page 111)*
- ___ large flour tortillas
- ___ softened cream cheese
- ___ assorted lunch meats and cheeses
- ___ colored paper

Peanut Butter Planks *(page 111)*
- ___ celery
- ___ peanut butter
- ___ raisins or chocolate chips

Buccaneer Banana Bread *(page 111)*
- ___ bananas
- ___ egg
- ___ butter
- ___ sugar
- ___ flour
- ___ salt
- ___ baking soda

Pirate Punch *(page 111)*
- ___ 32-oz can of pineapple juice
- ___ 12-oz can of orange juice concentrate
- ___ 6-oz can of lemonade concentrate
- ___ 1 quart 7-Up
- ___ 1 quart rainbow sherbet
- ___ punch bowl
- ___ orange, banana, kiwi, cherries (optional)

Walk the Plank *(page 112)*
- ___ 5' plank of wood
- ___ paper
- ___ pirate hat
- ___ cardboard

Pin the Pirate *(page 112)*
- ___ black construction paper
- ___ white chalk
- ___ drawing paper
- ___ double-sided tape
- ___ blindfold

Pass the Treasure *(page 113)*
- ___ 5 to 10 boxes of various sizes
- ___ wrapping paper
- ___ assorted candies or small prizes
- ___ music

Treasure Hunt *(page 113)*
- ___ small prizes and candy
- ___ small bags (optional)

Tales of the Seven Seas *(page 113)*
- ___ pirate-themed books

Treasure Chests *(page 114)*
- ___ small shoe boxes
- ___ self-adhesive paper, wrapping paper, or aluminum foil
- ___ decorating materials (e.g., plastic jewels, stickers, gold cord, shiny ribbons, sequins)

Pirate Ships *(page 114)*
- ___ Styrofoam bowls
- ___ craft sticks
- ___ white paper
- ___ basin of water (optional)

Pirate Hats *(page 114)*
- ___ black stiffened felt or foam paper
- ___ felt scraps in assorted colors
- ___ gold cord
- ___ feathers

Decorations and Miscellaneous
- ___ invitations and thank-you notes
- ___ plates, cups, napkins, and tablecloths
- ___ eating utensils
- ___ balloons, streamers, and confetti
- ___ party prizes and Treasure Chest fillers
- ___ pirate dress-up clothes
- ___ camera and film
- ___ music (optional)
- ___ beverages

Sleepover

BELT BAG PATTERN

(page 124)

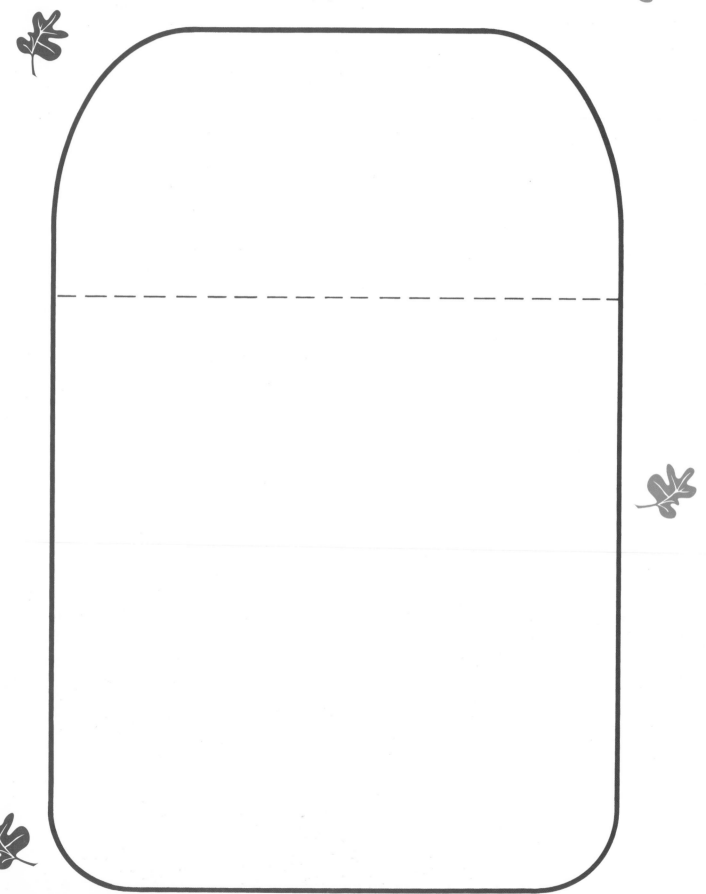

GETTING STARTED

A great party depends on successful planning. Use this handy guide to help you get ready for the best Sleepover Party ever! If weather permits, set up outdoor areas for games and activities. Kids will also enjoy playing and sleeping in backyard tents. Don't forget the flashlights!

One Month Before the Party
____ Decide on day, time, and location.
____ Write a guest list. (Keep the number manageable.)
____ Begin saving paper towel rolls for Make-Your-Own Telescopes.

Two to Three Weeks Before the Party
____ Make a tentative schedule of party activities.
____ Buy (or make) and send out invitations. Include an RSVP.
____ Make a list of decorations, food, and activity supplies.
____ Make or buy party decorations (e.g., banners, streamers).
____ Buy or make items needed for games and crafts.
____ Buy colorful party table items (e.g., paper plates, cups, utensils, tablecloth, napkins).
____ Buy food items that do not need to be refrigerated.
____ Buy treats and prizes.
____ Decide on indoor and/or outdoor areas for the games, crafts, food, sleeping, and gifts.
____ Select party music (optional).

Week of the Party
____ Finalize party schedule.
____ Call any guests who have not responded.
____ Buy last-minute food and party supplies.
____ Borrow tables, chairs, tents, and other needed items.

____ Prepare foods that can be made ahead of time (e.g., Campfire Cake, snack bags, Ants on a Log).
____ Cut out craft patterns and prepare a bag or box of materials for each craft.
____ Make sample crafts.
____ Make a cake or order one.
____ Order balloons.
____ Check CD or cassette player, video camera, and/or camera to be sure they're working.
____ Prepare all games and activities.

Day of the Party
Four hours before
____ Set the party table.
____ Pick up balloons and cake (if ordered).
____ Rent videos, if needed.
____ Set up games, crafts, and decorations.
____ Set up tents (optional).

One or two hours before
____ Complete last-minute foods and drinks.
____ Make sure your child is dressed for the party and ready to greet guests.
____ Organize music (optional).

As guests arrive
____ Greet guests and make them feel welcome.
____ Have paper and pen available to write down telephone or pager numbers where parents can be reached if needed.

CAMPFIRE CAKE

INGREDIENTS AND SUPPLIES

- cake mix of your choice
- prepared vanilla frosting
- green food coloring
- 1 cup of coconut
- 10 to 12 Oreo cookies
- miniature marshmallows
- chocolate sprinkles
- chocolate candies
- pretzel rods
- fudge ice cream
- candles
- two 8" round cake pans
- 2 resealable plastic bags
- rolling pin
- paper towel
- serving platter

There's nothing like a cozy Campfire Cake to set the mood for a night of fun and adventure. Add a scoop of fudge ice cream to top off this yummy treat.

DIRECTIONS

1. Mix, bake, and cool two 8" round cakes according to package directions.

2. To make "dirt," finely crumble the Oreo cookies by placing them in a resealable plastic bag and rolling over the bag with a rolling pin.

3. To make "grass," mix 1 teaspoon of water and a few drops of green food coloring in a plastic bag. Add coconut and shake well. Add more food coloring or water as needed to achieve the desired color. Spread the coconut on a paper towel to dry.

4. Add green food coloring to the vanilla frosting and ice the top of each cake. Place one cake on top of the other to form a two-layer cake. Frost the sides of the cake.

5. Sprinkle the cake with cookie dirt.

6. Place coconut grass around the top edge of the cake.

7. To build a campfire, arrange marshmallows, candies, sprinkles, pretzels, and candles as shown.

Party Foods

Campers will delight in these yummy vittles!

Party Kabobs

Ingredients and Supplies: frozen chicken nuggets, pizza bites, cheese bites, and/or other frozen snacks; miniature hot dogs; refrigerated breadstick dough; wooden skewers; bowls; baking sheet; knife

Directions

1. Thaw frozen snacks in the refrigerator overnight.

2. Cut breadstick dough into bite-size pieces.

3. Place snacks and dough in bowls, and invite children to alternate snacks and dough on their skewers.

4. Place the kabobs on an ungreased baking sheet and bake at 425° for approximately 10 minutes or until thoroughly heated.

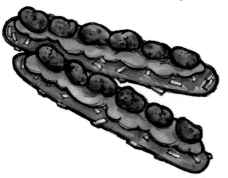

Ants on a Log

Ingredients and Supplies: pretzel rods, peanut butter, chocolate-covered raisins, knife

Directions

1. Spread one side of a pretzel rod with peanut butter.

2. Top the log with chocolate-covered raisins.

Breakfast Biscuits

Ingredients and Supplies: refrigerated biscuit dough, jelly or syrup, spoon, baking sheet

Directions

1. Separate biscuits and place them on the baking sheet.

2. Using a spoon, make an indentation in the center of each biscuit.

3. Fill the hole with jelly or syrup.

4. Bake the biscuits as directed on the package.

More Yummy Treats

Help children prepare individual snack bags to satisfy midnight cravings. Have some tasty ingredients (e.g., peanuts, raisins, popcorn, sunflower seeds, candy pieces) available for guests to scoop into sandwich-size resealable plastic bags. Write each guest's name on his or her bag with permanent marker.

S'mores are great nighttime treats! Sandwich milk chocolate squares and miniature marshmallows between two graham crackers and microwave on high for about 20 seconds.

GAMES AND

These races, relays, and other games add up to a festive night. Prizes, if any, should suit the age range of your guests as well as the theme of the party. Each child should receive several prizes. Consider stickers, pencils, small plastic toys, and other novelty items.

TIDDLYWINKS RACE

Materials: small plastic disks, paper plate, marker

Directions

1. Before the party, draw a silver-dollar-size circle in the middle of a paper plate.

2. At the party, set the plate on a flat surface.

3. Pass out four plastic disks to each guest.

4. Invite each child to snap three disks onto the plate by pressing the edges with another disk.

5. Write the child's name next to his or her best attempt (the disk that is in the circle or closest to it). Whoever lands the disk in the center or closest to the center wins.

Note: For larger parties, separate partygoers into two or three groups. Have a "snap-off" among the winners of each group to determine the grand snapper.

SLEEPING BAG BALL

Materials: 2 sleeping bags, beach ball

Directions

1. Unzip and open the sleeping bags.

2. Divide the partygoers into two groups. Provide each group with a sleeping bag.

3. Team members hold the edges of the bag and use it to toss the ball back and forth.

4. One team gains a point when the opposing team misses a toss.

5. The first team to earn ten points wins the game.

GOOFY GOO

Materials: gelatin, grapes, noodles, oatmeal, potato, blindfold, bowls, paper, pencil

Directions

1. Before the party, peel the grapes and potato, cook the noodles and oatmeal, and make the gelatin according to the package directions.

2. Place the items in separate bowls out of sight of partygoers.

3. Blindfold guests one at a time and invite them to guess what is in each bowl by smelling and feeling the contents. List their responses. Remind guests not to share their guesses with others.

4. After everyone has had a turn, read the list of guesses for each item before revealing the items. Give points for correct guesses. The child with the most points wins.

ACTIVITIES

SLEEPING BAG RELAY

Materials: 2 sleeping bags, 2 chairs

Directions

1. Clear a large area for the race. Set up chairs about 20 feet from the starting line and about 5 feet apart.

2. Divide the guests into two teams. The first player from each team steps into a sleeping bag and zips it up.

3. On *Go!*, the opposing players jump to the chairs, circle them, and jump back to their teams. The players then get out of their sleeping bags and give them to the next children in line to take a turn.

4. The team that successfully sends all its members to the chair and back first is the winner.

WHAT DID YOU SAY?

Materials: paper, pencil

Directions

1. Before the party, help the birthday child write three or four stories containing two sentences each. *(The pudgy pig loved pickles. He ate pickle sandwiches every day.)*

2. Invite party guests to sit in a circle. Have the birthday child whisper one of the stories to the next person in the circle. That child whispers it to the next.

3. The game continues until a parent or a helper writes down the story the last person whispers to him. The birthday child or helper reads the original story aloud and then the whispered version. Repeat the game, letting another child start the story.

DOUGHNUT DELIGHT

A great morning activity!

Materials: ringed doughnuts (1 per guest), string, bedsheet

Directions

1. Tie pieces of string through the doughnut holes.

2. Suspend the doughnuts from a clothesline or other high spot.

3. Place a sheet on the floor under the doughnuts to catch crumbs.

4. Line partygoers up in front of doughnuts with their hands behind their backs.

5. Players race to eat doughnuts without using their hands.

6. The first person to finish his or her doughnut wins the race.

SLEEPOVER CRAFTS

Delight your guests with these craft ideas. If you have room, prepare a separate table with a plastic tablecloth for your craft projects and supplies.

BELT BAGS

Materials: 8" x 10" sheets of brown felt (2 per bag), 2½" pieces of plastic string or yarn (1 per bag), buttons, belt bag pattern (page 118), party treats and prizes, hole punch, scissors, permanent marker, feathers (optional)

Directions

1. Use the pattern to cut two sides of the belt bag from felt squares. (The front of the bag ends at the dotted line. The back of the bag uses the entire pattern.)

2. Line up the front and back felt patterns so the bottoms match.

3. Punch holes about 1" apart around the bottom and sides of the bag. Do not punch holes around the flap.

4. Tie a button about 6" from the end of the string. Lace the bag.

5. After lacing up the bag, place the remaining button through the string and tie a knot about 6" from the end of the string.

6. Write a guest's name on each bag. Fill the bags with party treats and prizes, and fold the flap down. Before guests leave the party, tie each end of the string to a belt loop.

MAKE-YOUR-OWN TELESCOPES

You may decide to complete steps one, two, and three before the party, depending on guests' ages and time available.

Materials: paper towel tubes, 11" x 6" squares of posterboard, 5" squares of colored plastic wrap, paint, paintbrushes, rubber bands, tape, scissors, decorating materials (e.g., stickers, stamps, paper scraps, markers)

Directions

1. With a rubber band, secure a piece of plastic wrap to one end of a paper towel tube.

2. Tape posterboard around the paper towel roll to hide the rubber band and make the telescope more durable.

3. Paint the telescope and allow it to dry.

4. Decorate the telescope with various decorating materials.

CAMPING TENT

Materials: white prewashed flat bedsheet (queen size), fabric markers, foam stamps, paint, newspaper

Directions

1. Lay sheet on a flat surface. Place newspaper underneath working spaces to prevent markers from bleeding through.

2. Invite guests to draw camping scenes (e.g., campfires, animals, simple maps) and sign their names near their designs.

3. Turn the "camping collage" sheet into a tent by draping it over a table or several chairs.